A DOUBTER'S GUIDE TO THE TEN COMMANDMENTS

OTHER BOOKS BY JOHN DICKSON

A Doubter's Guide to the Bible
Hearing Her Voice, Revised Edition
Humilitas
Life of Jesus
The Best Kept Secret of Christian Mission
The Christ Files

A DOUBTER'S GUIDE TO THE TEN COMMANDMENTS

HOW, FOR BETTER OR WORSE, OUR IDEAS ABOUT
THE GOOD LIFE COME FROM MOSES AND JESUS | JOHN DICKSON

ZONDERVAN®

ZONDERVAN

A Doubter's Guide to the Ten Comandments
Copyright © 2016 by John Dickson

This title is also available as a Zondervan ebook. Visit
www.zondervan.com/ebooks.

Requests for information should be addressed to:
Zondervan, 3900 *Sparks Dr. SE, Grand Rapids, Michigan 49546*

Library of Congress Cataloging-in-Publication Data

Names: Dickson, John P., 1967- author.
Title: A doubter's guide to the Ten Commandments : how, for better or
    worse, our ideas about the good life come from Moses and Jesus /
    John Dickson.
Description: Grand Rapids : Zondervan, 2016.
Identifiers: LCCN 2015049556 | ISBN 9780310522591 (softcover)
Subjects: LCSH: Ten commandments — Criticism, interpretation, etc.
Classification: LCC BV4655 .D42 2016 | DDC 241.5/2 — dc23 LC record
    available at http://lccn.loc.gov/2015049556

Cover design: Studio Gearbox
Cover images: Thinkstock; Shutterstock
Interior design: David Conn

Printed in the United States of America

16 17 18 19 20 21 22 23 /DHV/ 20 19 18 17 16 15 14 13 12 11 10 9 8 7 6 5 4 3 2 1

For Edwin Judge,
who has inspired so many, including me, to read
ancient texts (Greek, Roman, and biblical)
and notice their impact on the
personality of the West.

CONTENTS

COMING HOME TO THE TEN COMMANDMENTS

The Ten Commandments are among the great cultural icons of the West. Even among those who can't quite list all ten, many say they "pretty much live by the Ten Commandments." They are probably right. The social impact of this ancient moral charter is so great that most people living in the West—even in my post-Christian Australia— *are* living by the Ten Commandments, pretty much. These rules seem to represent, consciously or not, what Westerners think of as the "Good" (as Socrates called it)—the happy union of the goal of human society and the virtues needed to get there.

Naturally, many Westerners prefer to say their vision of the Good is grounded in "secular ethical reasoning" (not religion), the sort of code any rational human being would aspire to under the right conditions. I don't believe that, and I hope I won't lose friends right here on the first page by saying that much of what is called "secular ethical reasoning" is just a *minor revision* of the Ten Commandments of Moses with a bit of Jesus of Nazareth thrown in.

These two ancient teachers have influenced us more than we might imagine. Like great-grandparents who fled a war-torn land to establish their family in an entirely new culture, Moses and Jesus have shaped our outlook and choices immeasurably, even if we don't know it. We may never have met them. Perhaps we've never even glanced at the "family tree." But we are their great-grandchildren. They are our heritage and our ethical homestead.

I am reminded of the great twentieth-century British thinker and writer G. K. Chesterton, who compared his philosophical journey to unwittingly discovering his own home. As an educated "free-thinker," as they used to call sceptics, he explored the world of ideas, confident that Christianity had very few of the important answers (or even questions). But when he stumbled across the intellectual and moral landscape he most admired, he was shocked to discover it looked like Christianity. He compared himself to an adventurous yachtsman determined to explore new frontiers, only to find that he had "discovered England under the impression that it was a new island in the South Seas." Finding Christianity was a mistake, he said, but a happy one: "What could be more delightful than to have in the same few minutes all the fascinating terrors of going abroad combined with all the humane security of coming home again?" (*Orthodoxy* [Image Books, 1959], 9–13). Like Chesterton, many thoughtful folk have walked away from the religion associated with their childhood, or with childishness per se, only to realise that some of their most mature "free thoughts" about justice, compassion, human rights, freedom, and so on are just an adult version of the Judeo-Christian worldview they thought they'd left behind.

Influential political philosopher Jürgen Habermas—who

remains an atheist—acknowledges the monumental cultural influence of Moses and Jesus. The West, he reckons, was shaped by the fairness ethic of Judaism and the compassion ethic of Christianity. "Egalitarian universalism," he says, "from which sprang the ideas of freedom, human rights and democracy, is the direct heir to the Judaic ethic of justice and the Christian ethic of love. To this day, there is no alternative to it" (Jürgen Habermas, *Time of Transitions* [Polity, 2006], 150–51).

Habermas's division between the "Judaic ethic of justice" and the "Christian ethic of love" is probably too neat (I'm sure he'd agree). It's not like Moses never talked about love nor Jesus about justice. But Habermas does put his finger on an important historical truth about the way the Ten Commandments came into Western culture. They arrived in *Christian* form. What I mean is that Judaism per se did not convert the West. Christianity did. And wherever Christianity went, the Jewish Scriptures, or Old Testament, complete with the teachings of Moses, also went. It was the specifically Christian vision of the Ten Commandments that gave the West its "egalitarian universalism," as Habermas puts it, its peculiar "ideas of freedom."

Throughout this book I will use the expression "Judeo-Christian" many times. For some it is a damaged descriptor, too heavily associated with right-wing politics or with a move to revive biblical law in legislation. Writing in Israel's *Haaretz* (26 Jan, 2015), Benjy Cannon offered a stinging reminder of how loaded and potentially exclusionary "Judeo-Christian" can be: on the lips of some, he says, it means little more than, *It's my America, not yours!* Jewish readers may also feel uncomfortable being lumped together with Christians! That's problematic. None of these connotations are intended in my use of the term. The expression has a long history, going back to the post-classical Latin *Judaeo-Christianus*. In English it has been with us since at least the 1800s as a technical description of beliefs—philosophical, ethical, theological—that are common to both traditional Judaism and traditional Christianity (but not shared by Greco-Roman culture). Hence the "Judeo-Christian view of God," or the "Judeo-Christian commitment to charity," and so on. It is important for me, both academically and personally, not to give the impression either that Christianity popped out of nowhere or to suggest that the church invented all the good things of Western culture. The Jewish background of Christian thought is vital for any accurate account of Western history. (And, yes, it is also true that Greece and Rome shaped Western civilization in many other profound ways: the term "Greco-Roman" is used for that influence. But that's for another book.)

All of this flags something important about the project of my book. While I will do my best to explain each of the Ten Commandments in their original Hebrew context, I wouldn't be doing you a proper service if I failed to explain how Moses's commandments were "transposed" by Jesus into a melody sung for almost two millennia now, the echo of which can still be heard in many contemporary discussions about what constitutes the Good. "Regardless of what anyone may personally think or believe about him," wrote Yale's Professor of History Jaroslav Pelikan in the famous opening sentence of his *Jesus Through the Centuries*, "Jesus of Nazareth has been the dominant figure in the history of Western culture for almost twenty centuries" (*Jesus Through the Centuries* [Yale University Press, 1999], 1). This is as true of art and culture as it is of philosophy and ethics.

Whether you are a believer or a doubter, I hope this book will provide more than an interesting account of the influence of the Ten Commandments in moral decisions. I trust you will find a little inspiration for the Good Life itself—a life that, according to Moses and Jesus, transcends mere morality and leads to an experience of genuine ethical *freedom*. The Ten Commandments may seem like an archaic, passé legal code with little relevance to modern life, but I hope I can show that this most ancient of Western traditions is as current as Google and Wiki—more so. As G. K. Chesterton once said in response to the claim that what is *current* trumps what is *traditional*:

> Tradition means giving votes to the most obscure of all classes, our ancestors. It is the democracy of the dead. Tradition refuses to submit to the small and arrogant oligarchy of those who merely happen to be walking about. All democrats object to men being disqualified by the accident of birth; tradition objects to their being disqualified by the accident of death. (*Orthodoxy* [Image Books, 1959], 48)

1
BIGGER THAN HAMMURABI, DELPHI, AND DAWKINS

Obviously, religious folk prize the Ten Commandments. My own mild-mannered Anglican tradition makes it one of just three requirements for those seeking Confirmation. According to the Book of Common Prayer, confirmees must know by heart — and *in the heart* — the Apostles' Creed, which is the oldest known affirmation of the Christian faith, the Lord's Prayer, which Jesus himself taught, and the Ten Commandments of Moses. Many other denominations give a similar priority to these basics.

THE SECULAR "TEN"

But the Ten Commandments also have a more public, secular face. Even in the land of the "separation of church and state" there is a large sculpture on the east pediment of the Supreme Court Building in Washington, DC, of Moses holding the two tablets of the commandments. He is flanked by Confucius, a representative of the Eastern tradition, and by Solon, an ancient Athenian lawgiver and poet (a nice thought: lawgiver *and poet*). But Moses is clearly given pride of place in this sculpture. The point of the display is not that the US Supreme Court is in the business of legislating the Bible (as much as some might want that). It is presumably just a cultural *nod* to the supreme and enduring impact of the teaching of Moses for the West's moral vision. The same can be said of the reliefs that circle the inside of the chamber of the US House of Representatives, where Moses appears in the middle, directly above the double doors. Eleven other historical figures appear to his left and eleven to his right, and he is the only figure directly facing the Speaker of the House and the only one *not* silhouetted. The symbolism is strong and deliberate.

So iconic are Moses's teachings that atheist groups have proposed their own "ten." Even Richard Dawkins in his *The God Delusion*, perhaps the most successful sceptical tome ever written, offers an approved list he found on an atheist website:

> Do not do to others what you would not want them to do to you.
>
> In all things, strive to cause no harm.
>
> Treat your fellow human beings, your fellow living things, and the world in general with love, honesty, faithfulness and respect.
>
> Do not overlook evil or shrink from administering justice, but always be ready to forgive wrongdoing freely admitted and honestly regretted.
>
> Live life with a sense of joy and wonder.

Always seek to be learning something new.

Test all things; always check your ideas against the facts, and be ready to discard even a cherished belief if it does not conform to them.

Never seek to censor or cut yourself off from dissent; always respect the right of others to disagree with you.

Form independent opinions on the basis of your own reason and experience; do not allow yourself to be led blindly by others.

Question everything.

Dawkins likes these, but says he would replace a few (I'm not sure which ones) with four further insights:

Enjoy your own sex life (so long as it damages nobody else) and leave others to enjoy theirs in private whatever their inclinations, which are none of your business.

Do not discriminate or oppress on the basis of sex, race or (as far as possible) species.

Do not indoctrinate your children. Teach them how to think for themselves, how to evaluate evidence, and how to disagree with you.

Value the future on a timescale longer than your own. (R. Dawkins, *The God Delusion* [Bantam Press, 2006], 263–64)

I find Dawkins's suggestions fairly unobjectionable and unremarkable, even if I'm not sure I want to stop discriminating between my children and my dogs.

CNN reported a recent competition to come up with the best set of godless guidelines. They were dubbed the "Ten Non-Commandments." The contest attracted nearly three thousand submissions, with $10,000 going to the winning combination. And here it is:

1. Be open-minded and be willing to alter your beliefs with new evidence.

2. Strive to understand what is most likely to be true, not to believe what you wish to be true.

3. The scientific method is the most reliable way of understanding the natural world.

4. Every person has the right to control of their body.

5. God is not necessary to be a good person or to live a full and meaningful life.

6. Be mindful of the consequences of all your actions and recognize that you must take responsibility for them.

7. Treat others as you would want them to treat you, and can reasonably expect them to want to be treated. Think about their perspective.

8. We have the responsibility to consider others, including future generations.

9. There is no one right way to live.

10. Leave the world a better place than you found it. (http://edition.cnn.com/2014/12/19/living/atheist-10 -commandments/)

The project is a fascinating thought experiment, and it reveals much about our age. There is something a little weird about calling these "*non*-commandments," when they are every bit as commanding as a biblical "thou shalt not." But such is our aversion today to the idea of rules for life— even though rules are among the most comforting and freeing elements of existence, as anyone who has tried to surf or sing or ski without instruction has quickly found. (More about this later.)

The first two prize-winning instructions above seem to be saying the same thing: follow evidence. They are probably designed to be snippy criticisms of some versions of religious faith. Ditto the emphasis on science in the third non-commandment: "The scientific method is the most reliable way of understanding the natural world." I hope the winning lawgiver means *how* the natural world *works*, because the scientific method tells us nothing about what the natural world *means*, or how we should *live* within it, or *why* living within it is worthwhile in the first place. Again, I suspect this (non-)commandment is just a little dig at perceived fundamentalist readings of Scripture. Fair enough.

More striking is the way several of these award-winning instructions resonate with the original Ten Commandments and with biblical ethics generally. "We have the responsibility to consider others" is pretty much what three or four of the Ten Commandments enshrine. And, "Treat others as you would want them to treat you" is a verbatim quote from Jesus in Luke 6:31. I wonder whether the winner and the organisers knew that, or if they all imagined they were recalling a principle of universal secular wisdom.

The final two commandments offer an almost humorous juxtaposition. Before earnestly mandating, "Leave the world a better place than you found it," the ninth rule declares without irony, "There is no one right way to live." A smart alec could be forgiven for asking, *If there is no one right way to live, why bother telling me to leave the world a better place than I found it? And what are the other commandments in this set about if not to guide me in the right way to live?* Then again, perhaps I'm being unfair and this ninth commandment just means there are a number of possible ways to properly obey all these rules. That would be true. But it's hardly worth making a rule.

All of this highlights a tension found in much atheist literature, from David Hume and Bertrand Russell to Richard Dawkins and Michel Onfray. On the one hand, there is a *philosophical admission* that universal morality is difficult to ground objectively if there is no absolute principle such as God, whose character establishes the Good. On the other hand, there is a *practical necessity* of articulating a moral viewpoint that doesn't sound like mere preference and that has the authoritative ring of religion about it without any of religion's justifications. The tension is perfectly, if unwittingly, illustrated in the ninth and tenth non-commandments above. The tension is not easily resolved. I will say more about this in chapter 4 when we look at the first commandment.

For now I am happy just to emphasise the iconic status of the Ten Commandments—in the priority given to them in our religious traditions, in the honour accorded to them in Western law, and even in the reverse compliment paid to Moses in recent atheist efforts to rewrite the Ten Commandments.

HAMMURABI, DELPHI, AND MOSES

The Ten Commandments, as taught by Moses and transposed by Jesus, are unquestionably the most renowned set of ethical statements in history. And I find it astonishing that Moses seems to have expected such an outcome. In a speech leading up to his rehearsal of the commandments, the great lawgiver declared:

> See, I have taught you decrees and laws as the LORD my God commanded me, so that you may follow them in the land you are entering to take possession of it. Observe them carefully, for this will show your wisdom and understanding to the nations, who will hear about all these decrees and say, "Surely this great nation is a wise and understanding people." (Deuteronomy 4:5–6)

This is remarkable. It's one thing to come up with guidelines that in the fortunes of history end up achieving international fame. It's quite another to predict such success the moment you lay the words down. It all must have sounded very implausible at the time, to some anyway. Whether prophetic or lucky, it is difficult to deny that Moses's expectation has been fulfilled on a fantastic scale. "The nations"—pretty much all of them—did indeed "hear about all these decrees."

The ancient world had some other very well-known moral codes, though I don't think any of them expected universal acclaim. The Code of Hammurabi, for example, is an astonishing collection of almost three hundred laws laid down by a Mesopotamian king (Hammurabi) in the 1700s BC, several centuries before Moses. The laws were inscribed on a large stele, or stone monument, and give early evidence of the regulation of inheritance, property, military service, marriage and divorce, and even banking systems, including an astonishing 33 percent interest rate on grain loans. Hammurabi was a great king, establishing an enormous empire through numerous important conquests. He certainly thought his code should be followed by future generations of Babylonians (which it wasn't), but he did not dare to imagine it would influence the world, and it didn't. Today, few have even heard of the great Code of Hammurabi.

The Maxims of Delphi provide another good example. Spectacularly important in sixth-century Greece yet virtually unknown today, this collection of 147 pithy imperatives is sometimes humorous and occasionally confronting: "Help your friends"; "Subdue pleasure"; "Pursue glory"; "Speak auspiciously"; "Nothing to excess"; "Rule your wife"; "Fear what controls you"; "Die for your country"; and on it goes. These aphorisms were thought ultimately to derive from the gods. Delphi itself, just north of Greece's Corinthian Gulf, was considered the epicentre of creation and a site of divine communication. But what was once considered the canon of ethical wisdom is now a subject of interest only to a subset of classicists and ancient historians. That's what *time* usually does to the moral creeds of humanity. (For more on the Delphic Canon or Maxims, see Edwin A. Judge, "Ancient Beginnings of the Modern World," in *Jerusalem and Athens: Cultural Transformation in Late Antiquity* [Mohr Siebeck, 2010], 282–314.)

The Laws of Hammurabi and the Maxims of Delphi are two of history's most famous moral codes, yet they enjoyed favour for a very limited time. Now they are all but forgotten. They have been eclipsed in a monumental way by ten simple "thou shalts" from a slave nation three thousand years ago. Pondering such a history makes a mockery of claims that biblical ethics is a thing of the past while secular ethical reflection, presumably of the kind articulated in the award-winning "Ten Non-Commandments," is the true future of morality. I doubt it. At least, we need a millennium or two to confirm it.

2 WHY BE GOOD?

There is a key question for all who ponder our theme: *Why be good?* What is the *motivation* for choosing one course of action over another? The Ten Commandments have some built-in answers, but I want to begin by confronting a widespread misunderstanding of this topic.

PUNISHMENT AND REWARD

In his book *Letters to a Young Lawyer* (Basic Books, 2001, 193–200) Harvard law professor Alan Dershowitz criticizes any religious motivation for morality as essentially *immoral*. The pious, he reckons, only "do good" to avoid eternal punishment and reap divine rewards. Hell and heaven provide the inspiration for ethics. This means religiously motivated behaviour is at its heart selfish. The atheist, on the other hand, is apparently free from all such fear or approval seeking and can pursue the good *for its own sake*. The unbeliever alone has a noble incentive for the Good Life.

Richard Dawkins follows suit. "Do you really mean to tell me the only reason you try to be good is to gain God's approval and reward, or to avoid his disapproval and punishment?" he asks of an imaginary believer pondering whether one can be good without God. "That's not morality," he insists, "that's just sucking up." (Richard Dawkins, *The God Delusion* [Bantam Press, 2006], 226). A slightly milder form of the same criticism comes from one of my favourite Australian social commentators, Hugh Mackay. In his aptly titled *The Good Life*, Mackay asks (and answers in the affirmative), "If a person is responding to the needs of others because they assume God will approve of their good behaviour rather than simply because those people are in need, is this not a rather tarnished, diminished version of goodness?" (Hugh Mackay, *The Good Life* [Macmillan, 2013], 186–187).

The criticism is misguided on several fronts. It caricatures religious motivation generally and disregards Christian motivation specifically. I wouldn't deny that the Bible does threaten punishment for bad behaviour and promise reward for good behaviour. We will find both in the Ten Commandments themselves. But what really is the problem with that? Society itself employs these motivations all the time. Professor Dershowitz of all people should appreciate this. It is in the very nature of our civil and criminal codes to punish wrongdoing and reward well-doing, and so to threaten and promise. There are penalties for driving at a hundred miles per hour in a sixty zone. And those penalties provide an effective reminder to drivers that speeding is usually a bad thing. The fear of a fine is a perfectly rational, if ultimately insufficient, motivation for keeping to the speed limit. It is not the complete incentive, for sure, but it is a reasonable one. We all know that the highest motivation for not speeding is *care for other drivers and pedestrians*, but no one would suggest that our road signs should therefore read simply: *Please slow down, lest you injure your fellow human being!* No. A simple number on a speed sign that evokes the threat of punishment is a shorthand reminder of appropriate behaviour in a civil society. Over time it directs our actions away from the bad and toward the Good. We all know what the Good is — not harming others — but the warning is sufficient in certain circumstances. We teach our kids in the same way. We all know there are higher moral reflections we hope our kids will one day appreciate, but fear of punishment gives the child a sense of drama appropriate to the weighty matter of ethical behaviour.

GRACE AND THE GOOD

In the Bible, however, *fear of punishment* and the corollary of *hope of reward* are patently *not* the key motivations for doing good. They are perfectly reasonable incentives in some circumstances, but they are not fundamental or sufficient.

So what are the key motivations for ethics in the Bible? One of the central inspirations for pursuing the Good is pretty much the inverse of *fear of punishment* or *hope of reward*. It is the knowledge that you are already loved and redeemed by the Almighty. Theologians call this the Doctrine of Grace, and it is everywhere in Scripture, including in the opening lines of the Ten Commandments themselves.

But first let me back up a little.

The Ten Commandments are a collection of laws given by Moses to the newly constituted people of God, Israel.

For centuries, the descendants of Abraham, the patriarch of the Jewish people, had been a slave nation in Egypt, where they were put to grueling work by despotic pharaohs. Moses emerged from among these Israelites to lead his people to freedom: he was the Martin Luther King of the second millennium BC Middle East. "Let my people go," was his plea to the Egyptian overlords, who finally acquiesced after a series of disasters sent on Egypt by the Creator (sometimes *fear of punishment* is the only motivation tyranny recognises).

After leading his people into liberty, Moses was called by God up Mount Sinai and given the laws we find in the Old Testament books of Exodus, Leviticus, Numbers, and Deuteronomy. The very first instructions were the Ten Commandments, what Old Testament scholar Chris Wright calls "the essential, constitutional core of the covenant" (Christopher J. H. Wright, *Deuteronomy* [Baker, 1994], 63). These ten rules were not just the first in a long list of Old Testament commandments (often numbered at 613). They have a special, guiding function in Old Testament law. Some experts, like Wheaton College's Professor John Walton, have even argued that the hundreds of rules that follow the Ten Commandments in the book of Deuteronomy are intentionally patterned around the Ten: the first commandment is unpacked in Deuteronomy chapters 6–11, the second commandment throughout chapter 12, the third commandment in chapters 13–14, and so on, so that the Ten Commandments are the founding principles behind the huge body of "case law" that follows (John H. Walton, "Deuteronomy: an Exposition of the Spirit of the Law," in *Grace Theological Journal* 8.2 [1987] 213–25).

My main point, however, is much simpler. The very first words of the Ten Commandments, before any imperative is issued, are about the fundamental motivation for all that follows. And they remind us of God's grace, his love set upon the Israelites *before* they had a chance to obey any of his wishes. The Ten Commandments thus begin:

> And God spoke all these words:
> "I am the LORD your God, who brought you out of Egypt, out of the land of slavery.
> (Command 1) You shall have no other gods before me.
> (Command 2) You shall not make for yourself an image." (Exodus 20:1–3)

The crucial point to observe is that the commandments begin with an unmistakable reference to God's prior saving action. He declares himself *already* "your God." He has *already* "brought you ... out of the land of slavery."

The observation is not arbitrary. There is a second biblical version of the Ten Commandments, and it emphasises the same thing. It comes from forty years later, just before Israel entered the Promised Land following decades of wandering. We find it in the book of Deuteronomy, meaning "second law." Moses reminds the Israelites of what God had asked of them at Sinai. There are some interesting differences between the two renditions of the Ten Commandments—I will point these out along the way—but the introductory sentence strikes precisely the same theme of divine grace preceding human morality:

> And he said:

"I am the Lord your God, who brought you out of Egypt, out of the land of slavery.

(Command 1) You shall have no other gods before me.

(Command 2) You shall not make for yourself an image." (Deuteronomy 5:5–8)

Even long-term believers sometimes assume that while Jesus and the New Testament highlight the theme of grace, Moses and the Old Testament underscore law. Occasionally Christians will talk as though Jesus came to save us from Moses! In reality, grace and obedience both appear in exactly the same relation throughout the Bible.

Numerous New Testament passages make clear that human good deeds are preceded and motivated by God's good grace. In one of my favourite texts, the apostle Paul reminds his colleague Titus, "When the kindness and love of God our Savior appeared, he saved us, not because of righteous things we had done, but because of his mercy." Two lines later he presents this as the motivation for good behaviour: "I want you to stress these things, so that those who have trusted in God may be careful to devote themselves to doing what is good" (Titus 3:4–5, 8). Salvation is not the reward for the Good Life; it is its inspiration.

The Old Testament emphasises the same theme. We have seen how both renditions of the Ten Commandments (in Exodus and Deuteronomy) make God's rescue of Israel the starting point for Israel's ethics. The identical point is made more subtly in the very organisation of the content of these two biblical books. The first we hear of any divine law is in Exodus chapter 20. But the first nineteen chapters tell the story of God liberating the nation from slavery in Egypt. The narrative structure is simple: from salvation to obedience.

Again, in the book of Deuteronomy — the second or reiterated law — commandments make up the bulk of chapters 5 through 34. But chapters 1 through 4 are a potted history of God's care for Israel over the previous forty years, from the rescue out of Egypt to God's protection from enemies and provision amidst scarcity. Moses reminds the people:

> The LORD your God has blessed you in all the work of your hands. He has watched over your journey through this vast wilderness. These forty years the LORD your God has been with you, and you have not lacked anything. (Deuteronomy 2:7)

And again:

> Because he loved your ancestors and chose their descendants after them, he brought you out of Egypt by his Presence and his great strength, to drive out before you nations greater and stronger than you and to bring you into their land to give it to you for your inheritance, as it is today. Acknowledge and take to heart this day that the LORD is God in heaven above and on the earth below. There is no other. (Deuteronomy 4:37–39)

You're loved. Now obey. This is the logic of biblical ethics. And we see it again in Deuteronomy 4, the section immediately preceding the introduction of the Ten Commandments. In an extraordinary passage, Moses simultaneously warns the nation of the consequences of disobedience *and* promises that, despite everything, God's grace will restore people after their rejection of his ways:

> After you have had children and grandchildren and have lived in the land a long time — if you then become corrupt and make any kind of idol, doing evil in the eyes of the LORD your God and arousing his anger, I call the heavens and the earth as witnesses against you this day that you will quickly perish from the land that you are crossing the Jordan to possess. You will not live there long but will certainly be destroyed. The LORD will scatter you among the peoples, and only a few of you will survive among the nations to which the LORD will drive you. There you will worship man-made gods of wood and stone, which cannot see or hear or eat or smell. But if from there you seek the LORD your God, you will find him if you seek him with all your heart and with all your soul. When you are in distress and all these things have happened to you, then in later days you will return to the LORD your God and obey him. For the LORD your God is a merciful God; he will not abandon or destroy you or forget the covenant with your ancestors, which he confirmed to them by oath. (Deuteronomy 4:25–31)

You're going to fail, Moses says, but God's grace will prevail. Here is a lovely reminder of the *ongoing* nature of divine mercy in the biblical tradition. Not only does God's mercy provide the motivation for behaviour, it also guarantees restoration following bad behaviour for all who "seek him." In the New Testament, this idea will come to a remarkable climax in the claim that Jesus Christ died, like an Old Testament sacrifice, for our past, present, *and even future* wrongdoing. He "atoned" for our sin, to use the language of the apostle John, one of the eyewitnesses of Jesus: "My dear children, I write this to you so that you will not sin. But if anybody does sin, we have an advocate with the Father— Jesus Christ, the Righteous One. He is the atoning sacrifice for our sins, and not only for our sins but also for the sins of the whole world" (1 John 2:1–2). According to the Bible, grace not only precedes our pursuit of the Good, it covers our failure to achieve the Good.

My goal is not to convince you that any of this is true. This is not that sort of book. I only want to emphasise an important feature of the structure of biblical ethics, one that is sadly misunderstood even by highly intelligent and informed folk like Professor Alan Dershowitz and his fellow biblical naysayers. The *fear of punishment* and a *desire for reward* do appear in the Bible among the various motivations for avoiding the bad and pursuing the Good. Quite right, too, for the reasons explained earlier. But no sensitive reader of the Old or New Testament could get the impression that this was the Bible's default incentive for moral conduct. Far more important throughout the Scriptures—and absolutely central to the Ten Commandments—is the thought that our actions are a grateful response to God's merciful actions toward us. As another key line from the apostle John puts it, "We love because he first loved us" (1 John 4:19).

3

THREE KEYS TO THE TEN COMMANDMENTS

Before unpacking the Ten Commandments in turn, I want to propose three keys for making sense of these hugely influential principles of human conduct. The first has to do with how the teaching of Jesus relates to the teaching of Moses, a theme hinted at in the Introduction. The second highlights the twofold structure of these ten instructions. And the third makes the counterintuitive point that the biblical "thou shalts" should be viewed as a kind of charter of freedom.

FIRST KEY: HOW JESUS "TRANSPOSED" MOSES

I said at the outset that the Ten Commandments exerted an influence on the world through the teaching of Jesus. It wasn't Judaism that spread throughout the nations converting people to biblical ethics (though certainly some conversion to Judaism took place in the Roman world); it was Christianity, with its extraordinary missionary activity. This is not a criticism of Judaism, by the way, and I imagine many Jews will take it as a compliment that I don't implicate them in

the *proselytising zeal* of New Testament faith. My point here
is simply the historical one: from the beginning it was the
specifically Christian interpretation of the Ten Commandments that took hold, first throughout the Middle East, then
throughout Europe, and on throughout Africa and Asia. Jesus
made Moses more famous.

I have written more books on the figure of Jesus than
I probably should have, so I won't labour a description of
his career here. I do, however, want to emphasise as clearly
as I can that Jesus claimed to be the *fulfilment* of Israel's
Scriptures. He wasn't cancelling one religion and starting
another. He said he was bringing the dreams of Moses and
the prophets of Israel to realisation. "Do not think that I
have come to abolish the Law or the Prophets," he said. "I
have not come to abolish them but to fulfill them" (Matthew 5:17). Reflecting on this twenty-five years later, the
apostle Paul taught his Roman readers, "Christ is the culmination of the law so that there may be righteousness for
everyone who believes" (Romans 10:4).

"Fulfilment" does not simply mean fulfilling Old Testament predictions—such as that the Messiah would be
born in Bethlehem, and so on. Jesus's concept of fulfilment
was richer. That's why Paul's word "culmination" is helpful.
Jesus is like the climactic scene of an epic piece of theatre.
His life, teaching, death, and resurrection resolve the ten-
sions in the story, crystalise the meaning of the story, and
take that story in directions only hinted at throughout the
body of the script.

None of this is a Christian invention after the fact. The
Old Testament itself points forward to a *new covenant* and

even a *new Moses*. The prophet Jeremiah, centuries *after* Moses and centuries *before* Jesus, announced:

> "The days are coming," declares the LORD, "when I will make a new covenant with the people of Israel and with the people of Judah. It will not be like the covenant I made with their ancestors when I took them by the hand to lead them out of Egypt, because they broke my covenant, though I was a husband to them," declares the LORD. "This is the covenant I will make with the people of Israel after that time," declares the LORD. "I will put my law in their minds and write it on their hearts. I will be their God, and they will be my people. No longer will they teach their neighbour, or say to one another, 'Know the LORD,' because they will all know me, from the least of them to the greatest," declares the LORD. "For I will forgive their wickedness and will remember their sins no more." (Jeremiah 31:31–34)

The Old Testament itself speaks of its inbuilt redundancy. Or perhaps the better way to put it is to say it points beyond itself.

Even Moses, seven hundred years before Jeremiah, told the Israelites that after his death a figure would stand in his place, a "new Moses" to whom God's people must pay close attention. In the middle of unpacking various laws about true and false prophets, Moses explains, "The LORD your God will raise up for you a prophet like me from among you, from your fellow Israelites. You must listen to him" (Deuteronomy 18:15). And just three lines later he basically repeats the point, saying that God had told him directly, "I will raise up for them a prophet like you from among their fellow Israelites, and I will put my words in his mouth. He will tell them everything I command him" (Deuteronomy 18:18).

The notion of a "prophet like Moses" is an important one. The closing lines of the book of Deuteronomy, written sometime after the death of Moses, tell us, "Since then, no prophet has risen in Israel like Moses" (Deuteronomy 34:10). Moses's own promise that a prophet like him would come, combined with the final editor's estimation that no prophet like Moses has in fact appeared, sets up a bit of speculation in the course of time about who the new Moses might be. At least three New Testament passages suggest that Jesus is the prophet like Moses, the one to whom people must pay special attention (John 5:46; John 6:14; Acts 3:19–22). The New Testament also explicitly says that Jesus founded the "new covenant" foretold by Jeremiah (Luke 22:20; 2 Corinthians 3:6; Hebrews 8:6–8).

This theological connect-the-dots has a simple point for now. Jesus "fulfilled" the Ten Commandments in his own teaching, and it was this rendition of Moses's instruction that shaped the Western world. To recall the analogy offered in the Introduction, Moses gave us a beautiful tune, which Jesus transposed into a melody that still resounds in many conversations about the Good Life today.

What I am calling Jesus's "transposition" of Moses sometimes had a dramatic effect on how particular lines of the Ten Commandments were heard and obeyed throughout history. For example, the instruction against fashioning divine images or idols (the second commandment) was, under the influence of Jesus, read as including a prohibition against pursuing material wealth at the expense of true

worship. The command about murder (the sixth commandment) was amped up to an extraordinary degree by Jesus
and the apostles to include the sin of anger and the refusal
to love others. I will say much more about this as we go.
The critical thing to note for now is simply that it was the
specifically Christian version of the Ten Commandments
that shaped Western ethics, and so moving from Moses to
Jesus, from old covenant to new covenant, is a key to fully
appreciating the remarkable impact of these ancient words.

SECOND KEY: THE TWO TABLES OF THE LAW

The second key is simpler and related. Both versions of the
Ten Commandments in the Old Testament tell us that these
commands first appeared not in a big book or on a large stele
(like the Code of Hammurabi or the Maxims of Delphi) but
on two simple tablets (Deuteronomy 9:15 – 17). The words
of the Ten Commandments are very few (less than two hundred), and we are probably to imagine quite small tablets. I
like to think of a couple of mini iPads. That there were *two*
tablets rather than one may symbolize that a copy belonged
to each party in the contract (Israel and God). But people
have often noted that the two tablets helpfully remind us
of the twofold structure of the Ten Commandments, what
people sometimes call the "two tables of the law."

The first four commandments concern reverence toward
God: serve him only; don't make images or idols; don't misuse his name; honour the Sabbath day. The following six
commandments (which happen to be expressed in fewer
words than the first four) are about respecting other human

beings: honour parents; don't murder; don't betray your spouse; don't steal; don't perjure yourself; don't covet what is your neighbour's. Honour the Almighty and care for your neighbour: that is the structure of the Ten Commandments. That is the twofold pattern of life that has shaped Western history in an irrevocable way.

Jesus saw things the same way, unsurprisingly. And he sharpened the focus a little. On one occasion he was asked a favourite theological question of the day: which is the greatest commandment of Moses. There were 613 to choose from (248 positive commands and 365 prohibitions), so it sparked quite a lot of debate in the period. Jesus did not hesitate to pick his two favourite quotations from Moses and present them as the sum total of the Good Life:

> Jesus replied: " 'Love the Lord your God with all your heart and with all your soul and with all your mind.' This is the first and greatest commandment. And the second is like it: 'Love your neighbour as yourself.' All the Law and the Prophets hang on these two commandments." (Matthew 22:37–40)

I find it interesting that Jesus refused to play the game in the way he was invited to. He was asked to name the "greatest commandment" *singular*. Just one. But Jesus did not think the law of Moses, the Good Life, could be reduced to one. So he offers two. The first comes from Deuteronomy 6:5, "Love the LORD your God with all your heart, etc.," the second from Leviticus 19:18, "Love your neighbour as yourself." I doubt Jesus was the only Jewish teacher to summarise ethics in this way, but a precise equivalent has not yet been found in the Jewish texts of the period.

Jesus thought the entire obligation of humanity could be summed up in a twofold imperative: love God and neighbour. This ties in perfectly with what we find in the two tables of the Ten Commandments, four commandments about devotion to the Creator, six about devotion to humanity.

This twofold obligation leaves little wiggle room, either for the *religious hypocrite* or the *moral agnostic*. The religious hypocrite is devoted to God but cold or complacent toward fellow human beings. It is an ugly type. We are right to deride it. Curiously, the Ten Commandments, especially in the crystallisation offered by Jesus, might equally call into question the inverse of this ugly type: the moral agnostic. On the logic of Moses and Jesus, the person who serves the neighbour but snubs the Creator is no more a "good person" than a hypocrite. We are all free to disagree with these iconic teachers. I suppose many do. I am just trying to tease out the structure of their thought. And, happily, most Westerners still do have a healthy regard for the Almighty. According to the *World Values Survey*, when asked, "How important is God in your life" (1 being "not at all important"; 10 being "very important"), 57 percent of Australians selected 6 or higher, with 28 percent selecting 10 (the figures are only slightly lower for Britain and significantly higher for the US). Such God-consciousness is not something you would pick up from our media or from conversations at the pub or café. It seems that even the "Godward" dimension of the Ten Commandments' vision of the Good is widely reflected in the secular West.

It could, of course, be argued that the logic of the two

tables is unfair; in fact, that it is illogical. "I don't believe in God," someone said to me when I recently tried to explain Jesus's inherent critique of the moral agnostic as much as the religious hypocrite. "So, how could I be morally obliged to pay him respect?" They went on, "But, obviously, human beings are all around me. I couldn't justifiably deny or ignore them!" It's a good point. The slight weakness, though, is that it assumes our "beliefs" in these matters are morally neutral. I doubt any of us really thinks that, deep down.

Take the example of Friedrich Nietzsche, perhaps the most influential and thoroughgoing atheist of modern history. The German polymath sincerely believed human beings were *not* all equal. The value of any particular man or woman arose from their strength of life and their (potential) contribution to the life of society. He had given up the idea that everyone, regardless of capacity or utility, was "created equal." There was no Creator. There was just the law of evolution, which, he insisted, selects the vigorous and discards the weak. It was on these grounds that Nietzsche despised the compassion ethic of Christianity, which he reckoned has "taken the side of everything weak, base, ill-constituted" (Friedrich Nietzsche, *Twilight of Idols / The Anti-Christ* [Penguin Books, 1990], 129–30).

So here's the question I put to my recent interlocutor: Was Nietzsche free from the moral obligation to show compassion to the weak simply because he did not believe in the doctrine of the equality of all humanity? Remember, my friend's logic was that because he didn't believe in God, there could be no obligation to revere God. I tried to point out that the same logic completely absolves Nietzsche (and his followers) from any commitment to the poor of mankind, something both of us could not bring ourselves to accept. Perhaps there is a way out of this conundrum for atheists. I don't pretend to have settled the matter. I'm just not sure that *not believing in God* lessens the universal claim of the Ten Commandments and Jesus that human beings have a twofold duty to revere the Creator and respect their fellow creatures. Or as Jesus put it, "Love God with all your heart" and "Love your neighbour as yourself."

THIRD KEY: THE CHARTER FREEDOM

But the Ten Commandments present themselves as far more than a "duty." They are a "charter of freedom," to borrow an idea from the previous book in this series (*A Doubter's Guide to the Bible* [Zondervan, 2015], 77). This is how they were read in their Old Testament context and also in the transposition of the New Testament. This is how they've been read for much of Western history, too. After all, the books of Exodus and Deuteronomy insist that this law of God brings "joy," "blessing," and "life." It is the way of freedom.

Our Jewish friends are right, then, to complain that the English translation "law" does not quite capture the essence of the original Hebrew term used throughout the books of Exodus and Deuteronomy, *torah*. Torah really means "instruction" and conveys the sense of being led along the way by an expert guide. The great ode to the Torah found in Psalm 119 in the Bible captures the thought well: "Great peace have those who love your law (*torah*), and nothing can make them stumble" (Psalm 119:165).

I realise the connection between "law" and freedom may seem counterintuitive, because today freedom is often understood as the *power to choose any course of action*. "Live and let live" is the only rule. Richard Dawkins echoes the sentiment in one of his own ten commandments: "Enjoy your own sex life and leave others to enjoy theirs."

Many talk like this, but we know it can't be right. Freedom cannot be the capacity to do whatever we choose, because some choices are destructive and enslaving — for ourselves and others. Think of the alcoholic, the workaholic, the pornography addict, or the friendless millionaire. Sometimes pure, unadulterated "choice" leads to a kind of servitude to our lesser selves.

"Freedom" is surely better defined as the *power to become what I am made for*. Few contemporary writers have put this better than American philosopher and theologian David Bentley Hart:

> In the more classical understanding of the matter, whether pagan or Christian, true freedom was understood as something inseparable from one's nature: to be truly free, that is to say, was to be at liberty to realize one's proper "essence" and so flourish as the kind of being one was. ... [W]hatever separates us from that end — even if it comes from our own wills — is a form of bondage. We become free, that is, in something of the same way that (in Michelangelo's image) the form is "liberated" from the marble by the sculptor. This means we are free not merely because we can choose, but only when we have chosen well. For to choose poorly, through folly or malice, in a way that thwarts our nature and distorts our proper form,

is to enslave ourselves to the transitory. (*Atheist Delusions* [Yale University Press, 2009], 24–25)

The law or *torah* of God was originally thought of in precisely this way: it was the path out of "slavery to the transitory," into the life the Creator intended for his creatures. Hence the great refrain throughout the book of Deuteronomy following many of its instructions: "that it might go well with you" (Deuteronomy 4:4; 5:16; 5:29; 6:3; 6:18; 8:16; 12:25; 12:28; 22:7). One of these appears in the Ten Commandments themselves, in the fifth commandment:

> Honour your father and your mother, as the LORD your God has commanded you, so that you may live long and that it may go well with you in the land. (Deuteronomy 5:16)

Undoubtedly, the promise that all would "go well" is related to the specific agreement, or "covenant," God established with Israel. According to Exodus and Deuteronomy, God promised his people fruitful abundance in the promised land if the Israelites responded to his grace by trusting his guidance or *torah*. This was specific to the old covenant. It would be inappropriate to apply this beyond its context, as some "prosperity gospel" preachers do when they promise health, wealth, and happiness to all who "follow Jesus." I am not even sure I can go along with Michelle Bachman, the former Minnesota Republican member of the US House of Representatives (and one-time Presidential hopeful), who in her farewell address to the House in 2012 declared that "the Ten Commandments that God gave to Moses is the very foundation of the law that has given happiness and the rise of the greatest prosperity that any nation has known before" (http://www.rawstory.com/rs/2014/12/michele-bachmann-god-gave-moses-the-ten-commandments-so-america-would-be-rich/).

Still, there is a valid principle in the promise "that it may go well with you," one that ties into Bentley Hart's description of the classical notion of freedom as "the liberty to realize one's proper 'essence' and so flourish as the kind of being one was." There is blessing in obedience.

I take my lead from the apostle Paul in the New Testament. In his letter to the Ephesians, he cites the fifth commandment, making a point of its promise of blessing:

> Children, obey your parents in the Lord, for this is right. "Honour your father and mother"—which is the first commandment with a promise—"so that it may go well with you and that you may enjoy long life on the earth." (Ephesians 6:1–3)

Paul knows the Ephesians are not living in the land of Israel (they're all in Turkey, after all!). He has also just been telling the Ephesians that they are not living under the old covenant of Moses (Ephesians 2:15). And, yet, the apostle can still happily quote the fifth commandment *and* its promise of blessing. There is a principle that seems to continue into the new covenant.

Paul expresses a similar idea in 1 Timothy 4:7–8, written to one of his missionary colleagues in the early 60s of the first century AD: "Train yourself to be godly. For physical training is of some value, but godliness has value for all things, holding promise for both the present life and the life to come." The apostle doesn't think "godliness"—i.e., living by God's guidance—benefits only the future. He insists it "holds value" right here and now in the messy rough-and-tumble of human existence.

Living God's way puts us in harmony with his world and with his purpose for our lives. God's ways *work* like a manufacturer's instructions work. This mustn't be turned into a mechanical formula; we are right to be unnerved by the prosperity preachers. Until God's future kingdom, of which the promised land was a preview, things will fail. Obedience to God's ways will often bring a cost and lead to suffering. Try saying otherwise to the oppressed Christians throughout Iraq and Syria today. And, yet, we can say that God's ways, embodied in the Ten Commandments and transposed in the teaching of Jesus, are what human beings are made for. The Good Life is "good" because it corresponds to our nature and purpose as creatures intended by the Creator.

With these three keys in place we are ready to begin unpacking the Ten Commandments themselves, conscious of the way the teachings of Moses have come into the West through the teachings of Jesus, sensitive to the twofold challenge to love God and neighbour, and open to the possibility that this ancient charter draws us into the liberty of living out our intended form. These things don't need to be believed in order to get something out of the Ten Commandments, but they do need to be held in mind—if only heuristically—to appreciate the timeless allure of this *torah*.

4

ONE GOD AND THE GOOD:
FIRST COMMANDMENT

The first commandment is a call to take God seriously.

I am the LORD your God, who brought you out of Egypt, out of the land of slavery. You shall have no other gods before me. (Exodus 20:1–2; Deuteronomy 5:6–7)

At the heart of biblical faith is *monotheism*, the conviction that there is one God over all things. Some ancient cultures held to *polytheism*, the acceptance of multiple deities worthy of worship. Others expressed what is called *henotheism*, the belief that one deity rules as chief of the gods — in the Greek pantheon this status was held by Zeus. Monotheism is strikingly different, and quite rare in antiquity, and it has huge consequences for one's view of the world and one's approach to ethics.

Debate continues over whether the Israelites were pure *theoretical monotheists*, believing that *only* the God of Israel exists, or whether they were *theological monotheists*, holding that, while other spiritual beings or gods may be said to exist in the world, only Israel's Lord was the source of everything, standing alone over creation as the ground of all things.

Whichever kind of monotheism is the more accurate description of Israel's God, the first commandment insists that no other "gods," whether real or imagined, are to be given any airtime. No gods "before me" does not mean *given priority over me*, as if God were just asking for preferment! It literally reads, "on or against my face," an expression meaning "in my presence." Since the God of Israel was thought to be present *everywhere*, this command is absolute. Having "no gods in my presence" is really an emphatic way of banishing all notions of deity, save the God of Israel.

Monotheism is not simply the Bible's first command; it is its very first subject. The opening line of the first book of the Bible reads: "In the beginning God created the heavens and the earth" (Genesis 1:1). This is not merely a sensible way to start a holy book. It is a swipe at all ancient notions of deity. In the ancient Near East it was commonplace to believe that many gods were involved in the production or fashioning of the created order. Divine status was given to thunder, sea, sun, moon, and so on. These things were reverenced not just as majestic physical features of the cosmos but as spiritual powers in their own right which need to be placated. (See my *Doubter's Guide to the Bible* [Zondervan, 2015] for more details on this and on how to read the controversial early chapters of Genesis.)

Genesis 1:1 proclaims an emphatic *No* to all ancient cosmologies. By giving the production of "heaven and earth" to a single actor, God, the author of Genesis leaves nothing in the universe for any other deity to do. Monotheism is not just the Bible's first commandment, it is its first thought.

CAN YOU BE GOOD WITHOUT GOD?

Devotion to *one God* is more than a rarefied theological vision. It is the foundation of biblical ethics. It grounds the way of life the Bible envisages for humanity. Monotheism and morality are intimately linked. Only if there is a coherent, ultimate reality imprinted on the world can there be objective moral principles — a way of life that aligns us with reality and a way of life that does not.

Before we turn to atheism, think for a moment of the widespread polytheism common when the Bible was written. If the world is the result of a *potpourri* of different forces, as polytheism holds, we may be able to placate the individual deities, but there is no way to align our lives to a coherent, ultimate reality — for in polytheism there is no such reality. This is partly why in ancient Near Eastern, Greek, and Roman religions, there was no direct link between *spiritual* beliefs and practices and *moral* beliefs and practices. It was left to the philosophers, particularly people like Aristotle, to try and work out what our ethical obligations might be. And Aristotle's great work *Ethics* has surprisingly little reference to the formalities of Greek religion. Religion was a separate category of thought for him. Today, we take for granted that religion and ethics are intimately associated, but this is one of those deep — and therefore almost imperceptible — cultural influences that comes from Judaism (and which Christianity and Islam inherited).

Atheism likewise cannot provide a rational basis for objective morality, and for pretty much the same reason as polytheism. If there is no coherent, ultimate reality imprinted on the world, there can be no way to align your life to a coherent, ultimate code of behaviour. This is dangerous territory, I realise. It is nearly impossible to talk about the logical link between God and ethics without people, sometimes my own friends, anxiously putting a stop to the conversation: "You can't possibly be saying you need religion to be good. Many atheists are as kind as the best Christians!"

So let me acknowledge upfront that I do *not* think one needs religion to be good. I also believe that atheists can be every bit as kind as believers, more so even. The case I want to pursue has nothing to do with the *capacity* for goodness in believers versus unbelievers. If readers get to the end of the chapter thinking I do in fact think that the religious are better than the irreligious, please accept my apology and put it down to my failure to communicate the subtle idea in my head.

My claim is that moral principles cannot be considered *universal* (applicable everywhere) or *objective* (true regardless of who approves it) unless there is a God whose character is the logical ground of universal, objective moral principles. Again, I am not saying that one cannot act *as if* moral principles are universal and objective, only that such an outlook is not logically coherent unless there is a Universal Being responsible for the creation of the world.

For thoroughgoing atheists like Friedrich Nietzsche, this point was not controversial. He accepted that the "death of God" meant the death of objective, universal ethics. He has been followed in this respect by many atheist thinkers, including the influential Oxford philosopher J. L. Mackie in his classic *Ethics: Inventing Right and Wrong* (Penguin,

1991), and more recently by Richard Joyce in *The Myth of Morality* (Cambridge University Press, 2007).

None of these thinkers says atheism leads to immorality. Their case is the theoretical one: Where there is no Absolute Being, moral principles cannot be considered objective. Without God, morals are really just social conventions or individual preferences. We assign an objective status to these conventions in order to stress their importance, but we cannot argue that they have the true-false status we normally assign to facts. This is not just because we lack enough evidence to declare one action "good" and another action "bad." It is because the very concepts of good and bad—without God—are not factual elements of the world at all. The statement "X is morally right" really just means "I prefer X and want you to like X as well." But as soon as you meet someone who declares, "I dislike X," the atheist has very little to say by way of objective argument. On the atheist's own assumptions, "X" is not a behaviour corresponding to an ultimate reality. It is a social convention or something believed to be beneficial to people.

Take the example raised in the previous chapter. Nietzsche did not believe that pity towards the weak was rational. What could his fellow atheists possibly have said to him to argue otherwise? Sure, they might try the argument that a society in which people care for the poor and needy is one in which more people could survive and thrive, but he might well reply that such a society was not preferable (to him) over one in which the stronger and more skilful people tend to survive and thrive and pass on their traits to strong and skilful offspring. What would an interlocutor's next move be?

He could perhaps pull out the bold affirmation, "But, Herr Nietzsche, all human beings are inherently and inestimably precious; they have inalienable rights!" But Nietzsche would surely reply, "Who says?" at which point his fellow atheist has nothing to say. Even on his own assumptions, the concept of a human being's inalienable rights is arbitrary. It does not connect with any universal or objective truth about the universe. Contrast this with the imaginary conversation a Christian philosopher might have with Nietzsche. It would surely climax in the statement, "Human beings are inestimably precious because God, as the source of all things, has made this creature in his image." Nietzsche would, of course, say, "Rubbish!" and the conversation would end! But my point is that the Christian, on his own assumptions, can not just *feel* that human beings are inherently valuable; he can *rationally defend* the proposition on his own assumptions. The atheist, on the other hand, can only *feel* his conclusion. He has nothing logical to say (on his own assumptions) to the person who does not share the feeling.

Richard Dawkins comes close to acknowledging this. In his oft-quoted article from twenty years ago:

> In a universe of blind physical forces and genetic replication, some people are going to get hurt, other people are going to get lucky, and we won't find any rhyme or reason in it, nor any justice. The universe we observe has precisely the properties we should expect if there is at the bottom no design, no purpose, no evil, and no good; nothing but blind, pitiless indifference. DNA neither knows, nor cares. DNA just is, and we dance to its music. (*The Telegraph*, London, Wednesday, May 10, 1995)

In his 2006 *God Delusion*, Dawkins spends a good part of his chapter six ("The Roots of Morality: Why Are We Good?") complaining about religious folks who think God is the ground of the Good. But then, in a throwaway line toward the very end of the chapter, he acknowledges, "Nevertheless, it is pretty hard to defend absolutist morals on grounds other than religious ones" (232). And, indeed, he makes no effort to make such a defence himself. The closest he comes is earlier in the chapter when he argues that morals are a by-product of our evolution from early human village life. Kindness, empathy, altruism, and so on, were all traits that evolved to assist individuals in tight communities to survive and pass on their genes. These urges to compassion are, Dawkins says, "just like sexual desire. We can no more help ourselves feeling pity [*Nietzsche aside!*] when we see a weeping unfortunate (who is unrelated and unable to reciprocate) than we can help ourselves feeling lust for a member of the opposite sex (who may be infertile or otherwise unable to reproduce). Both are misfirings, Darwinian mistakes: blessed, precious mistakes" (*God Delusion*, 221).

Sam Harris in his *Letter to a Christian Nation* argues similarly. Describing the Ten Commandments as unremarkable, he states:

> There are obvious biological reasons why people tend to treat their parents well, and to think badly of murderers, adulterers, thieves, and liars. It is scientific fact that moral emotions—like a sense of fair play or abhorrence of cruelty—precede any exposure to Scripture. Indeed, studies of primate behaviour reveal that these emotions in some form precede humanity itself. All of our primate

cousins are partial to their own kin and generally intoler-
ant of murder and theft. They tend not to like deception
or sexual betrayal much, either. Chimpanzees, especially,
display many of the complex social concerns you would
expect to see in our closest relatives in the natural world.
(*Letter to a Christian Nation* [Knopff, 2006], 21–22)

Even if Dawkins and Harris were right about the evolutionary origins of the moral instinct, they must recognise
that this makes no contribution at all to the question of
whether one course of action is *good* and another *evil*. Presumably, human and primate instincts for revenge, selfish-
ness, rape, and violent domination *also* evolved to convey
some survival benefit to our early ancestors. But the evolutionary history of revenge, for example, tells us precious
little about whether *revenge* is good or bad in any given context, just as the evolutionary history of *pity* tells us nothing
about its moral status. Explaining the physical origins of
an instinct is not the same as providing a rational basis for
evaluating it.

Nor is it enough to say, as Harris goes on to say, "For
there to be objective moral truths worth knowing, there
need only be better and worse ways to seek happiness in this
world. If there are psychological laws that govern human
well-being, knowledge of these laws would provide an
enduring basis for an objective morality" (*Letter to a Christian Nation*, 23–24). Science, in other words, can tell us
what things increase human happiness, and *that's* a solid
basis for morals. But there's a gap in the argument. Who
determined that "happiness" ought to be the goal? That is a

very twenty-first-century American offering. Other societies have insisted that "honour" was the great Good. Others claimed it was "duty." Still others "power." So, even if we could scientifically measure the human sense of happiness, honour, duty, or power, this would tell us nothing about which of these was the right goal to pursue in the first place. Worse for Harris's argument, even if we accepted "happiness" in the broad sense as the great Good, different cultures through history would have located the sources of happiness in quite different realities: *philosophy* for ancient Greece, *victory* for ancient Rome, *comfort* or *pleasure* in the modern West, *racial ascendency* in Nazi Germany, and so on. In other words, the scientific measures of happiness-enhancement in Plato's Athens would not be the same as those in twenty-first-century Sydney! Worse still, none of this would tell me why I should seek to accrue this Good — whether happiness, honour, or whatever — for anyone beyond my "tribe." Why should I seek the Good for someone on the other side of the planet whose life has no impact on my own? Harris may reply: because I intuitively feel it. But that doesn't help. Many *don't* feel it. Many others feel the contrary. And so we are back to the original problem. How do we rationally assess one "moral emotion," as Harris calls them, over another?

A friend of mine recently pointed all this out on the official Facebook page of the *Richard Dawkins Foundation for Science and Reason*. He was deleted and permanently blocked. My friend did present his case in a rather stark fashion, but it was an astonishing response from the moderators. Here is what my friend posted in its entirety:

Atheists don't believe people are a special or privileged species. In other words, we are no different to slugs. [Okay, so my friend should probably have made clear that he knows most atheists don't feel or act like humans are no different from slugs!] When atheists (like Stalin) treat people like slugs, they are being quite consistent with their philosophy. [Again, I wish he'd made plain that he knows most atheists don't follow Stalin's approach.]

Christians do believe people are special and privileged. We are God's "children," and have inherent value and dignity. When we treat others badly, we are being "inconsistent" with our philosophy.

"Love your neighbor" doesn't follow logically from atheism. It's not integral to that philosophy. It does follow logically from Christianity, and is absolutely integral.

If "There is no God," then "Love your neighbor" is optional.

If "Christ is Lord," then "Love your neighbor" is fundamental.

As I say, my friend probably put things too bluntly. He should have made clear that atheists and Christians are equally capable of love and hate. Still, his intellectual point is difficult to overturn. He is not denying that most atheists are just as ethical as most Christians. He is just observing that, on atheist assumptions, no course of action flows more logically than another. When an atheist hates, she is neither logically following nor defying her atheism. When she loves, she is neither logically following nor defying her atheism. Not so for someone who believes that at the core of the universe there is a God of love, whose own character provides the logical guarantee of love. When a Christian hates, she is logically defying her Christianity. When she loves, she is logically following her Christianity.

Here is what I mean by monotheism and morality being connected. The existence of God, out of whose own character the universe has been made, establishes the universal and objective nature of moral actions. Some actions are good to the degree that they reflect the reality of his character imprinted on the world. Some actions are bad to the degree that they shun that imprint.

By the way, all of this happily resolves a question sometimes put to religious believers as a riddle. It is called the "Euthyphro dilemma" and it goes back to a conversation between Socrates and Euthyphro. *Are actions good and just because God wills them, or does God will them because they are good and just?* The answer is: *yes*, or perhaps *no*. In biblical logic, God is the source of all things. If existence itself is derived from his will, it follows that there is an absolute correspondence between God's good character and what is objectively *good* in the universe. Jonathan Sacks, the former chief rabbi of Britain and a formidable public intellectual, speaks for Jews and Christians when he declares, "In Judaism, the Euthyphro dilemma does not exist" (*To Heal a Fractured World: The Ethics of Responsibility* [Schocken, 2007], 162). Things aren't good simply because God commands them. Nor is there some higher charter of the Good, to which God himself is subject. No. It is simply that God exists, and his character is the ground of all the world's Good.

IS MORALITY JUST COMMON SENSE?

It is not enough to say, as one of my favourite commentators does, that this kindness ethic is "common sense":

> Virtually every philosophical and religious tradition (to say nothing of our common sense) tells us, with the clarity and urgency of a ringing bell, that there's only one good way for humans to live. If we want to contribute to a civil society by promoting the peaceful, harmonious and mutually supportive communities which are our natural habitat, we must learn to treat other people in the way we ourselves would wish to be treated—the so-called Golden Rule. (Hugh Mackay, *The Good Life* [Macmillan, 2013], 1)

As a historical statement, it is just false to say that most traditions have affirmed the Golden Rule. No one who knows the history of Egypt, Babylon, Greece, or Rome could say such a thing. I wonder if the Golden Rule feels like "common sense" to an educated Westerner like Hugh Mackay because the Golden Rule shaped the culture in which he lives. I know that attempts are often made, including by Mackay, to find parallels to the famous saying of Jesus, "Do unto others as you would have them do unto you," but the parallels are few and have only a semblance of similarity. Confucius, for instance, said, "Do not inflict on others what you yourself would not wish done to you" (Confucius, *Analects* 15.23). But any similarity is in the grammar not the moral vision. The difference between the negative "do not inflict harm on others" and the positive "do unto others" is the difference between my trying not to hate you and my deciding to love you, between my resisting the urge to punch you in the nose and my building a hospital for you.

We live in a culture that imbibed the Golden Rule because for much of our history a majority of citizens thought there was a God whose character was reflected in the Rule. Nowadays, fewer people believe in such a God but we still hold the moral viewpoint it inspired, as a kind of cultural echo. We maintain the ethical stance without the ground it once stood on. It is "common sense" only because its rationale was once very common. "What we possess," said the great Catholic (former Marxist) moral philosopher Alasdair MacIntyre, "are the fragments of a conceptual scheme, parts which now lack those contexts from which their significance derived." We have what he terms "simulacra of morality," and "we continue to use many of the key expressions." But we have largely lost the logical ground upon which these expressions—such as "Do unto others"—once rested (Alasdair MacIntyre, *After Virtue* [Bloomsbury Academic, 2007], 2–3).

Important atheists, like J. L. Mackie mentioned earlier, say the same thing. The philosopher and atheist Raimond Gaita has put it particularly well:

> Only someone who is religious can speak seriously of the sacred, but such talk informs the thoughts of most of us whether or not we are religious for it shapes our thoughts about the way in which human beings limit our will as does nothing else in nature. If we are not religious, we will often search for one of the inadequate expressions which are available to us to say what we hope will be a secular equivalent of it. We may say that all human beings are

inestimably precious, that they are ends in themselves, that they are owed unconditional respect, that they possess inalienable rights, and, of course, that they possess inalienable dignity. In my judgment these are ways of trying to say what we feel a need to say when we are estranged from the conceptual resources we need to say it. Be that as it may: each of them is problematic and contentious. Not one of them has the simple power of the religious way of speaking. (Raimond Gaita, *Thinking about Love and Truth and Justice* [New York: Routledge. 2002], 23–24)

Again, thinkers like MacIntyre, Mackie, and Gaita, and many others, are not suggesting that a loss of belief in God leads to a loss of morals. But they are saying that without God our ethics can no longer be considered objective and universal. A new way of talking about "right" and "wrong" is thus needed, on their view.

For my part, I am happy to stick with the old view contained in the Ten Commandments and the teaching of Jesus. God created the world out of his own character. Our actions can therefore be right or wrong depending on how they reflect or defy that character.

In short, the first commandment ("you shall have no other gods before me") is *first* not just because it concerns the first priority (our Creator) but also because it grounds all the other commandments in a coherent reality. Anyone who sincerely adheres to the one God described in the Bible has a deeply logical reason for naming some things good and some things bad. These are not a matter of local preference or the vote of the majority, but a reflection of ultimate reality.

5
IDOLS OF THE HEART:
SECOND COMMANDMENT

Given the importance of monotheism for an objective, universal vision of morality, it is no surprise that the next two of the Ten Commandments concern *taking the one true God seriously*. Reducing God to an idol (the second commandment) or trivialising his name (the third commandment) has potentially disastrous consequences for Israel's picture of the Good Life. The first three commandments, then, not only pay due honour to the Creator — crucial in itself — but also guarantee the moral vision of his creatures.

I love to tell a story of three young men on a bus in Detroit in the 1930s who tried to pick a fight with a stranger sitting quietly by himself at the rear. After not responding for several minutes, the mysterious man stood up. He was much, much larger than he had seemed. He simply handed the lads his business card and walked casually off the bus and on his way. The card read: *Joe Louis. Boxer.* They had just tempted fate with the future Heavyweight Boxing Champion of the World. I don't know if the tale is true — it ought to be — but I have often wondered about the truth it emphasises. How we evaluate a person surely affects the way we treat them and how we behave in their presence.

The second and third commandments bear out this insight. How we value God's nature and name shapes how we approach him and live in his world. One doesn't need to share the theology of Moses in order to appreciate the function of the Ten Commandments, but one should at least understand it.

GOD IS NOT A GOD

The second commandment is intended to preserve the "otherness" of God. Making God in our own image is such a persistent danger of the human mind—ancient and modern—that Israel's Lord forbade any such attempt and attached to it one of the sternest warnings imaginable:

> You shall not make for yourself an image in the form of anything in heaven above or on the earth beneath or in the waters below. You shall not bow down to them or worship them; for I, the LORD your God, am a jealous God, punishing the children for the sin of the parents to the third and fourth generation of those who hate me, but showing love to a thousand generations of those who love me and keep my commandments. (Exodus 20:4 – 6; Deuteronomy 5:8 – 10)

I will discuss the dire warning in these verses—punishment "to the third and fourth generation"—at the end of the next chapter, after having fully explored the second *and* third commandments. Both are about taking God seriously, and both are connected to this threat and promise. But first, *idols*.

Ancient pagans *divinized* everything—the sun, the moon, the sea, the earth, and so on. All of these were seen as divine relics. This was as true for ancient Egyptian worship of the sun (*Ra*) as it was for ancient Indian or Germanic worship of storm gods (*Indra* or *Thor*). It would be tempting to think that this made everything "special," turning simple physical elements into objects of wonder and delight. In fact, it made everything unpredictable and potentially dangerous. As a consequence, it fostered an oppressive superstition, where magical solutions were desperately sought in order to tame the capricious forces of the world.

The ancient Israelites divinized nothing. They thought of the material world *not* as a magic charm or *totem* to be feared and placated, but as a work of art from the hand of a benevolent Artist. It was separate from the Artist but it reflected his character. The words "it was good" appear as a refrain (seven times) throughout the Bible's opening chapter, climaxing with the emphatic "God saw all that he had made, and it was *very* good" (Genesis 1:31).

This separation between *God* and his *creation* is one of the key thoughts of the Bible and a philosophical dividing line between Judaism (and later Christianity and Islam) and all ancient Near Eastern, Greek, and Roman visions of deity. But it is also one of the most obvious missteps of contemporary (popular) atheism. You will sometimes hear Richard Dawkins, Sam Harris, Lawrence Krauss, and others speak of the "Christian God" as just another competitor in the endless roll call of gods through history—Marduk, Zeus,

Indra, Wotan, Thor, and so on. We are told that a Christian's unbelief toward, say, Wotan, the great Norse deity, is no different from the atheist's rejection of all the other gods, including the biblical one. Since the reasons for believing in the biblical God are no more sound than those for believing in Nordic gods, so the argument goes, Christians really ought to dismiss *one god more* and embrace atheism.

At this point atheists are making a category error. And I am confident no philosophically informed atheist who also knows about the history of religion would go along with the line. Wotan, Zeus, Indra, Ra, and the rest, are all supernatural creatures *within creation*. Scepticism about them is akin to scepticism about fairies or the Loch Ness Monster. There is no particular reason for such creatures to exist. It is just that people say they exist. We look for any trace of evidence and find that such evidence is not forthcoming—to the satisfaction of most, anyway. The God of the Bible is another species entirely. By definition, the biblical God is outside of creation and outside of time. Otherwise, he could not be the source of space-time. He is the eternal mind responsible for existence itself. God, in other words, is not a god at all.

Dawkins and others are looking for God like he's a magical wardrobe hidden somewhere in the house of creation. But the Bible describes him more like the Architect of the house itself. Atheists are running through each room of the house gleefully declaring the absence of the wardrobe, all the while missing the more telling fact that there is a house, complete with rooms and doors and hallways, in the first place. Philosopher and theologian David Bentley Hart puts the point starkly, contrasting belief in fairies and gods with belief in God:

Beliefs regarding fairies are beliefs about a certain kind of object that may or may not exist within the world, and such beliefs have much the same sort of intentional shape and rational content as beliefs regarding one's neighbors over the hill or whether there are such things as black swans. Beliefs regarding God concern the source and ground and end of all reality, the unity and existence of every particular thing and of the totality of all things, the ground of the possibility of anything at all. Fairies and gods, if they exist, occupy something of the same conceptual space as organic cells, photons, and the force of gravity, and so the sciences might perhaps have something to say about them, if a proper medium for investigating them could be found.

... But all the classical theological arguments regarding the order of the world assume just the opposite: that God's creative power can be seen in the rational coherence of nature as a perfect whole; that the universe was not simply the factitious product of a supreme intellect but the unfolding of an omnipresent divine wisdom or logos.... According to the classical arguments, universal rational order—not just this or that particular instance of complexity—is what speaks of the divine mind. (David Bentley Hart, *The Experience of God: Being, Consciousness, Bliss* [Yale University Press, 2013], 33–38)

None of this is offered as a proof of God's existence. I am really just underlining the great chasm that exists between pagan deities and the biblical notion of God. Anyone who wants to place these two items in the same intellectual basket really needs to ponder why the most learned philosophers in the world today—whether atheist or theist—write massive tomes weighing up the various arguments for God, while never so much as mentioning "the problem of fairies" or "arguments for Wotan." The existence of God provides a powerful explanation of why there is something rather than nothing, why the universe has the character of mathematical beauty and order instead of chaos, and why the universe has produced minds like ours that are able to ponder such matters. Fairies, on the other hand, explain nothing.

All of this explains why the Bible is so dogmatic in its rejection of idol worship. Idolatry dethrones the one true God who stands outside and over creation, and it relegates him to a merely mysterious and powerful feature of creation itself, like a fairy. It turns God into a god. To take a piece of creation and worship it—whether the sun in the sky or an idol made with human hands—is to give the Artist's glory *to his art*. Idolatry, in other words, insults the power of God by redefining the very nature of God. An idol is a speechless, lifeless, actionless item of the world. It could never represent the speaking, life-giving, action-packed Lord of all creation. This is the logic of the second commandment.

IDOLS OF THE MIND

A friend recently put a fresh thought in my head about all of this. As a Muslim, Darya agreed with the biblical rejection of physical images of God. Judaism, Christianity, and Islam all share this "iconoclastic" approach to idol worship. Her problem with Christianity, however, was the New Testament claim that Jesus is more than a teacher or prophet; he is *God in the flesh*. Is this not just another idol, she wondered, a finite image of limitless deity? This is a common Islamic critique of Christianity. But as Darya was reading the great Oxford thinker C. S. Lewis one day, another perspective took hold. Perhaps it is possible to create *mental* images of God — theological dogma — which are human constructs of divinity just as much as any idol crafted from wood or stone. "It makes little difference whether they are pictures and statues outside the mind or imaginative constructions within it," Lewis writes in *A Grief Observed*. "My idea of God is not a divine idea. It has to be shattered time after time. He shatters it Himself. He is the great iconoclast."

God is the great iconoclast. As Darya pondered the idea, she came to wonder if her own cultural resistance to the idea of God becoming a human being was itself a theoretical idol that had to be smashed. She opened herself up to the possibility that God could, if he so determined, choose to make himself known personally, bodily. Who was she, Darya told to me, to hold onto a mental picture of the Creator that forbade him to enter his own creation — the Architect turning up at the house. God smashed her idol and it was a significant step in her careful intellectual journey to a vibrant Christian faith today.

The specifics of Darya's story are unusual, but it raises a broad and important question for many of us today — who are not tempted to worship physical idols. A majority of Westerners continue to believe in the existence of God: for most, it seems inherently likely that the universe's *living energy* and *rational order* have their source in a Powerful Mind. But, beyond this, what of our mental constructs of God? What popular idea of divinity do I hold onto, and why? Do I imagine God as only ever smiling on me with approval? Or do I perhaps think of God frowning on all and sundry? Do I picture a God who wound up the universe in the beginning and let it go? Or perhaps I see God as pulling every string like a puppeteer? Any of these ideas of deity could be mere constructs, the result of my personal preference or a cultural fashion.

This is not to say that we cannot, in principle, have an accurate idea of God. If God chose to reveal himself, it would be intellectual idolatry to *refuse* such a self-disclosure (that was Darya's point). What I am saying is that I want my picture of God to be open to critique. As a Christian, this means I want to submit my imagination, and my preferences, to the biblical portrait of the Creator. For those who don't share my faith, it may just mean remaining open to the possibility that their ideas about God are "imaginative constructions," as Lewis put it.

Atheists will, of course, say that the very idea of God is an imaginary, superstitious construct. God himself is an idol. I would reply that it cannot be "superstition" to hold that the rational order of the universe and corresponding rationality of human consciousness are grounded in a Timeless Mind. That is surely a rational move of the purest kind (whether or not it turns out to be true). It provides a complete explanation of rational order and conscious mind without itself requiring an explanation, since, by definition, God is eternal. He doesn't need to arise from anything prior to himself. Surely the more superstitious viewpoint today is the doctrine that rational intelligibility and conscious mind arose from exactly nothing, just like magic. Atheism may, in fact, be the greatest example of an idol—a mere human mental construct that dethrones mind itself. In any case, we can perhaps all agree that it cuts all three ways: the Christian theist, the general theist, and the atheist may be creating and adhering to their own mental portraits of deity.

HOW IDOLATRY DIMINISHES HUMANITY

Idolatry does more than demote God to a feature of his creation. Idolatry diminishes *us*. According to the first book of the Bible, there is just one "image" of God on earth, a divine representative. It is humanity itself. The climax of the creation narrative in Genesis puts this in no uncertain terms, repeating the idea over and over:

> Then God said, "Let us make mankind in our *image*, in our *likeness*, so that they may rule over the fish in the sea and the birds in the sky, over the livestock and all the wild animals, and over all the creatures that move along the ground." So God created mankind in his own *image*, in the *image* of God he created them; male and female he created them. (Genesis 1:26–27)

The closest thing God has to an "image" on earth is us—men *and* women. Worshipping a material object, then—to go back to the default idea of idolatry—doesn't just insult God, it diminishes humanity. After all, if you can relegate the eternal Creator to a mere material object, it is a small task to objectify some of his creatures. J. R. R. Tolkien gives us a picture of this in *The Lord of the Rings*. The once human (well, humanoid "hobbit") Gollum finds himself trapped by his lust for his "precious," a magical ring that promises to increase power and extend life. Slowly but surely Gollum himself is degraded as he treats others as means to his insatiable ends. In elevating a mere object to God-status, he is able to demean everything else. Tolkien, himself a thoughtful Christian, was presumably alluding to the danger of pursuing *things* at the expense of genuine existence.

It is perhaps by a similar logic that the Bible sometimes links *idolatry* to *injustice*. In Deuteronomy 12, just a few chapters after the Ten Commandments, Moses warns of the dangers of the surrounding idol-worshipping cultures, which bow down to images and "burn their sons and daughters in the fire as sacrifices to their gods" (Deuteronomy 12:31).

Elsewhere in the Bible, the prophets frequently criticise God's own people, Israel, for two great sins: elevating images to divine status and denigrating human beings as commodities. The prophet Ezekiel, seven hundred years after Moses, sees idolatry and injustice as intertwined. He castigates the "evil man" in the words:

> He eats at the mountain shrines. He defiles his neighbour's wife. He oppresses the poor and needy. He commits robbery. He does not return what he took in pledge. He looks to the idols. He does detestable things. He lends at interest and takes a profit. (Ezekiel 18:11–13)

If you can downgrade the Creator to a handmade object of wood or stone, you can easily treat humans as objects of convenience. If, on the other hand, you see God as supreme, above all representation, and humanity as bearing the sacred status of his "image," you could never *validly* oppress other human beings. Pristine monotheism ought to lead to a benevolent humanism that pays honour to all, regardless of capacity or utility, as inestimably precious creatures, even children, of the Source of all existence.

HOW GREED IS IDOLATRY

The theme of idolatry is taken in a curious direction in the New Testament. From the beginning of this book I have emphasised the way Jesus transposed the Ten Commandments through his own teaching. It was this Christocentric rendition of the words of Moses that spread throughout the Western world and continues to exert an influence. The second commandment provides a good case in point. But, first, another analogy.

I have already compared Jesus's reflections on the teaching of Moses to a musical transposition or key change. Another way of thinking about it is as a "refraction" of light, an analogy explored in the previous book in this series (*A Doubter's Guide to the Bible*, 83–85). When a beam of light passes through a transparent prism, the various electromagnetic waves that make up the appearance of colourless light change speed and so bend apart giving the appearance (to the human eye) of different colours. A rainbow is a naturally occurring refraction. Some readers may be able to picture the front cover of Pink Floyd's classic album *Dark Side of the Moon*—where a single ray of white light passes through the left side of a prism and comes out the other side as red, orange, yellow, green, blue, and purple (it's worth Googling, and the album is definitely worth hearing!). In any case, if you think of the teaching of the Ten Commandments as a ray of white light passing through the prism of Christ—his life, death, and resurrection—you have a helpful mental picture of the transformation that takes place in the new covenant. The "new Moses" refracts the light of the first Moses, making some things clearer, some things more intense, and others transformed almost beyond recognition. When we discuss the fourth commandment (the Sabbath day) we will see an example of a radical transformation. But the first and second commandments provide examples of refraction as *intensification*. Jesus saw these commands as extending to the problematic human tendency to *revere the stuff of creation* over the Creator himself. Money can become a "god." Greed can become idolatry.

In a passage of the Sermon on the Mount, Jesus first warns against trusting in the god of money—or "mammon," as older translations have it—and urges his followers to rely on the true God and Creator of all:

> No one can serve two masters. Either you will hate the one and love the other, or you will be devoted to the one and despise the other. You cannot serve both God and money. Therefore I tell you, do not worry about your life, what you will eat or drink; or about your body, what you will wear. Is not life more than food, and the body more than clothes? Look at the birds of the air; they do not sow or reap or store away in barns, and yet your heavenly Father feeds them. Are you not much more valuable than they? (Matthew 6:24–25)

The word "money" in the expression "serve both God

and money" is not the term we would expect in a document written in Greek (*argurion*, "money/silver"). Instead, what appears in the Greek manuscripts is a transliteration of the Aramaic term for wealth, *mamona*—hence the "mammon" of old translations. This has the effect of almost personifying wealth, especially in a sentence contrasting *mammon* with "God." Identical words appear in Luke 16:13. The Gospel writers are drawing attention to the way money, according to Jesus, can become a sort of deity which people "love" and "serve" as "master," three words the original audience would have associated with God, the true Master worthy of our love and service.

Thirty years after Jesus, the apostle Paul highlighted a similar theme in his New Testament epistle to the fledgling Christians of Colossae in southwestern Turkey. He explicitly describes the pursuit of material wealth as "idolatry":

> Put to death, therefore, whatever belongs to your earthly nature: sexual immorality, impurity, lust, evil desires and greed, which is idolatry. (Colossians 3:5)

Greed and *idolatry* may sound like two completely different things. But there is a real connection. Both involve our devotion to created things rather than to the Creator. As I have argued elsewhere, "although our pursuit of the material is hardly a conscious act of 'worship,' it is often a deliberate substitute for 'worship.' It's as if we hope that the accumulation of numerous smaller 'meanings' will make up for the lack of a grand meaning—as if the sum of the material parts will be greater than the spiritual whole" (*If I Were God, I'd Make Myself Clearer* [Matthias Media, 2002], 22).

Here is where the Bible offers a healthy perspective which, to a lesser or greater degree, has shaped the Western approach to wealth for centuries and which deserves reflection even today. The stuff of creation is a definite *good*. Genesis 1 repeatedly emphasises this point. We call them "goods" for a reason. But when material things dominate our affections, even challenging our creaturely love for the Creator, they become "idols." And, of course, just as old-fashioned idol worship can lead to human injustice, so can the idolatry of greed. If we can replace the good Creator with the goods of creation, we can very easily commoditize other creatures, seeing them as means to material ends. And we see it every day, as the bottom line drives ethical decisions, as people pursue careers at the expense of relationships, as corporates crush small businesses because "it's just business," as first-world luxuries come at a cost to the conditions of third-world factory workers, and so on. In this sense, the words "you shall have no other gods before me" and "you shall not make for yourself an image" continue to have something to teach even the most secular of cultures.

6

TAKING RELIGION SERIOUSLY: *THIRD COMMANDMENT*

The third commandment, no less than the first two, seeks to preserve the dignity of God. If God exists, this is a worthy goal in itself—no less important than a parent teaching a child to show respect. But there is probably another dimension. Like a good parent, God knows that the fidelity of his children to him is a key to their own flourishing. The concern for the divine "name" in the third commandment can be viewed as an end in itself and as a guarantee of human welfare. Who could deny that the misuse of God's name, and of religion generally, has been a source of misery through history? And so Moses declares:

> You shall not misuse the name of the LORD your God, for the LORD will not hold anyone guiltless who misuses his name. (Exodus 20:7; Deuteronomy 5:11)

The words of the third commandment literally read, "You shall not take up the name of Yahweh your God to worthlessness"; hence the more memorable King James Version, "Thou shalt not take the name of the LORD thy God in vain." Pausing a little on the literal words opens up important insights.

GOD'S CRYPTIC NAME

First, "Yahweh"—usually appearing as the uppercase LORD in modern translations—was the *personal name* God revealed for Israel to use in worship. According to the book of Exodus, when God appeared to Moses at a "burning bush" calling him to lead the Israelites out of Egyptian slavery, Moses queried whether others would accept his authority without knowing the name of their ancestral God. The reply was cryptic but significant:

> Moses said to God, "Suppose I go to the Israelites and say to them, 'The God of your fathers has sent me to you,' and they ask me, 'What is his name?' Then what shall I tell them?"
>
> God said to Moses, "I AM WHO I AM. This is what you are to say to the Israelites: 'I AM has sent me to you.'"
>
> God also said to Moses, "Say to the Israelites, 'The LORD, the God of your fathers—the God of Abraham, the God of Isaac and the God of Jacob—has sent me to you. This is my name forever, the name you shall call me from generation to generation.'" (Exodus 3:13–15)

The passage is intriguing and many interpretations of the details can be found in the scholarly literature. For our purposes the basic facts will do. The Hebrew lines translated above repeat the simple verb "to be" (*hyh*). In the grammatical first person this appears as "I AM" (*ehyeh*). After using the "I AM" verb three times, the above text then employs a word translated by the capitalised "LORD." This must be distinguished from the lower case noun "lord," which renders a different Hebrew term. Underlying the capitalised "LORD" above is the Hebrew term *Yahweh*, a version of the "to be" verb. *Yahweh* recalls the two "I AM" verbs hitched together at the beginning of the verse, where God says of himself, "I AM WHO I AM." It is awkward but emphatic. God's forever name is *Yahweh* and he is who he is.

There is debate about what exactly this "I AM" business means. Some take it *philosophically*, so that God is being described as the ground of all existence. Others see it as a statement of *presence*—God is everywhere, always. Still others read *Yahweh in light of the earlier* "*I AM WHO I AM*," seeing it as a *promise* of faithfulness, as if to say "I will be there for you." And so on. But why not *all* of the above, and more? The expression is so cryptic, and certainly not a typical personal name, that it is possible it is deliberately expansive and multivalent. We're talking about *God* after all!

Whatever the precise philological and philosophical details of the word *Yahweh*, the most important point of the narrative, and of the third commandment, is that God invites Israel to know and address him not as Distant Majesty but as Personal Being, someone with a name. Revealing a name, then as today, is often a gesture of intimacy. Imagine the current President of the United States urging you to call him Barak (which I understand not even his closest advisers will do), or the Queen of England saying, "Call me Lizzy!" which I imagine no one does!

The name of God is considered so special in modern Judaism that an Orthodox Jew (and some others) today will not even say it out loud. In the *Siddur*, the Jewish Prayer Book used in public and private worship, wherever the divine name *Yahweh* appears in the Hebrew text, the worshipper says instead "*Hashem*," which means "the Name." In my copy of the *Siddur*, which has facing English-Hebrew pages, the opening prayers of the morning, for instance, read, "Blessed are You, *Hashem*, our God, King of the universe.... May it be Your will, *Hashem*, my God and the God of my forefathers.... Bless *Hashem*, O my soul; *Hashem* my God, You are very great."

One way never to take up God's name in vain is never to say it. But the third commandment means more than this simple act of reverent avoidance of the divine name. What exactly does it mean to "misuse the name of the LORD your God" or, more literally, to "take up the name Yahweh to worthlessness"?

Naturally, the modern use of "God," "Jesus," and "Christ" as substitute swear words could be a form of taking the Lord's name in vain. I suppose it depends on what's in the mind of the speaker. Yet, even this is not what the third commandment targets directly.

There are two related ways in which ancient Jews might "take up" the name Yahweh on their lips, and potentially do so worthlessly.

SPEAKING TRUTHFULLY IN GOD'S NAME

First, many scholars see the third commandment as specifically about *swearing oaths* using the sacred name of God. Thus, Old Testament scholar Bruce Wells writes, "The prohibition of the third commandment likely targets those who might swear false judicial oaths in the name of Yahweh — to lie under oath, as it were" (John Walton, ed., *Zondervan*

Illustrated Bible Backgrounds Commentary, vol.1 [Zondervan, 2009], 232). Israelites were to be truth-tellers, especially when making promises or speaking in court. The name of God was never to be employed as a "cover" for lies — as a means of heightening the *appearance* of truth-telling while getting away with lies.

Significantly, Jesus banned oaths altogether: "But I tell you, do not swear an oath at all: either by heaven, for it is God's throne; or by the earth, for it is his footstool; or by Jerusalem, for it is the city of the Great King. And do not swear by your head, for you cannot make even one hair white or black. All you need to say is simply 'Yes' or 'No'; anything beyond this comes from the evil one" (Matthew 5:34 – 37). Perhaps this provides an example of the "refraction" of the *torah* beyond recognition. The third commandment forbade lying under a divine oath. Jesus pushed this same logic to its final end point: truth-telling is so important that an oath — in the name of God or anything else — should not be necessary. And since oaths employing the divine name were sometimes used as a cover for deceit, the practice itself should be excluded. This is not really a contradiction of the third commandment but its ultimate fulfilment.

What might this mean in a modern context, where judicial oaths and promises are *not* really taken in the personal name of the God of Israel? Presumably, one of the main ways the third commandment is broken today is in the false teaching of religious leaders. When church officials mislead their people in the name of God, employing the Lord's credibility as a cloak for corruption, we are observing a very real example of a breach of God's ancient *torah*. Such leaders ought to reflect carefully on the warning attached to the commandment, "the LORD will not hold anyone guiltless who misuses his name."

HYPOCRITICAL WORSHIP IN GOD'S NAME

There is another context in which Israelites would "take up" the name Yahweh on the lips, and it perhaps has even more contemporary bite. Leaving aside the modern avoidance of saying "Yahweh" in Jewish worship, God's name was "taken up" throughout the Old Testament in prayers, songs, and sacrifices. In the biblical Psalms we read, "I will praise you as long as I live, and in your name I will lift up my hands" (Psalm 63:4), or "I will lift up the cup of salvation and call on the name of the LORD ('Yahweh')" (Psalm 116:13). To "lift" one's "hands" or "cup" in the "name" of the LORD is to worship the One who disclosed himself personally to Israel. It is likely the third commandment targets not only false oaths in the name of Yahweh, but also *phoney* displays of reverence for God and, as some scholars suggest, even the use of God's name as a magical device, an incantation to manipulate events (a common enough practice in ancient pagan religion).

In our context, to take up the name of the LORD in vain is to go through the motions of worship, to trivialise our approach to God, or to use prayer like a good-luck charm. Old Testament specialist Chris Wright draws this out in his comments on the third commandment:

> Then there is the equally trivialised use of God's name in the commercialisation of religion, whether by the

> overt forces of mammon or by the more subtly damaging
> forces of organised religious empires, the 'televangelists'
> ... with their prosperity gospel and unscrupulous mar-
> keting of hopes and promises.... By 'giving God a bad
> name' — i.e., by blatantly using God's name in the inter-
> ests of their own selfishness, power, or pride — they are
> in principle breaking the third commandment. (Wright,
> *Deuteronomy*, 74)

I will never forget my first experience of the all-American TV evangelist. I had seen comedy sketches of the figure, but nothing really prepared me for the real thing. It was my first trip to the US. I was tired, turned on the television, and was greeted by a man with a beautiful southern accent dressed in a stylish suit. "God is a God of prosperity," he told me. "He wants to bless your life with the house and car of your dreams." I was so surprised I got out the dictaphone I used to carry everywhere and pressed record. He had a special deal going this particular day. He had "prayer cloths," which looked to me like a tea towel for drying dishes. Because he'd prayed over them, the cloths could bring blessing to any home that possessed one. He promised to send one to every viewer "free of charge" — I kid you not — "with every $1000 donation"! To prove that the magic worked he showed us footage of his own home and car collection. Sure enough, they were large and spectacular! Everything about this man's performance seemed like a flouting of the third commandment. He was trivialising and commercialising God's name. He was employing it as a cover for falsehood — and even for magical purposes. (He was later exposed and imprisoned for fraud.)

Throughout the course of history divine names have been employed for thousands of similar examples of false-hood and superficiality. This was par for the course in pagan religion, where the important part of worship was the external performance of ritual and where worshippers had a principally *transactional* relationship with priests, holy men, temple prostitutes, and the like. Unfortunately, the religion of Moses or Jesus isn't immune from the same trivialisation of spirituality and the misuse of the divine name for false purposes.

But within Judaism and Christianity there is at least an in-built critique of such hypocrisy, which has little parallel in pagan religion. The third commandment completely forbids the worthless use of God's name for petty human ends. Jesus railed against those who put on a show of religion: "Woe to you, teachers of the law and Pharisees, you hypocrites! You give a tenth of your spices — mint, dill and cumin. But you have neglected the more important matters of the law — justice, mercy and faithfulness" (Matthew 23:23). The first petition of the prayer Jesus taught his disciples, the so-called Lord's Prayer or Our Father, says "Hallowed be your Name." No one who sincerely prays for God's name to be "hallowed," that is, *revered* or *considered holy*, could at the same time use the trappings of faith for selfish, trivial, or deceitful ends. At least in theory.

People commonly criticise the church for making a "show" as a cover for bad behaviour. They are right to do so. But it is worth noting that attacking hypocrisy is not a recent secular invention, the result of the Enlightenment or anything like that. Nor can it be traced to ancient Egyptian,

Babylonian, Greek, or Roman religion. It comes from Moses and from Jesus, whose criticisms of religious hypocrisy were stinging and frequent. This gave divine permission to Western culture ever since to expose all pretences of faith. There is no doubt that Christians have often failed to live up to many of their own values; it's the topic of a future book in this series, *A Doubter's Guide to Church: How Christians Have Been Better and Worse than You Ever Imagined*. But within Christianity itself there are deep resources for self-critique. There is a sacred duty to shun and expose all *vain* and *worthless* uses of God's name.

At the close of the first "Christian millennium," when parts of Christian Europe had settled into patterns of power and luxury, people like St. Odo (927–942), the second Abbot of Cluny in eastern France, emerged with their powerful denunciations of wealthy Christendom: "How then are these robbers Christians, or what do they deserve who slay their brothers for whom they are commanded to lay down their lives? If we judged by realities we should give honor not to the rich for the fine clothes they wear but to the poor who are the makers of such things — for the banquets of the powerful are cooked in the sweat of the poor" (*Collationes*, III, 26–30). The critiques and reforms coming out of Cluny influenced Europe from Southern Italy to Eastern England, and inspired similar tenth-century movements that accused Christendom of hypocrisy and dragged the church back to its own ideals (St. Gerard, St. Bavo, St. Omer, St. Bertin, et al.). Eventually, some of these reformers were elected pope (Leo IX in 1048; Gregory VII in 1073), and the overhaul of Christendom became official policy.

On the crucial influence of medieval Christianity for the development of Western culture, see the classic by Christopher Dawson, *Religion and the Rise of Western Culture* (Doubleday, 1991).

BOOK NOTES

Much, much more could be said about these periodic movements of reform within the church, but my larger point is simple: exposing hypocritical religion is part of Christianity's own heritage. It is built into the fabric of the faith itself. The modern secularist attack on religious hypocrisy, commercialisation, and trivialisation is not a "secular" activity at all. It is a thoroughly *Christian* enterprise, whose origins are found in the third commandment and which can be traced all through Christian history. As painful as public critiques of Christian hypocrisy can be, I often find myself secretly thanking God for the gift of the reformers and the opponents of the church. They are frequently doing God's bidding, in the tradition of Jesus himself.

THE PROBLEM OF PUNISHMENT

The third commandment ends with a vague reference to punishment for taking up the name of Yahweh in vain: "for the LORD will not hold anyone guiltless who misuses his name" (Exodus 20:7). The statement is brief and nondescript perhaps because it is meant to recall the lengthier and more dramatic warning that appears at the end of the second commandment:

85

> For I, the LORD your God, am a jealous God, punishing the children for the sin of the parents to the third and fourth generation of those who hate me, but showing love to a thousand generations of those who love me and keep my commandments. (Exodus 20:5–6)

The first three commandments, as I have said, are about taking God seriously. The penalty for not doing so is also serious, even though we're not told what that punishment involves. What is the logic?

If you compare God's "jealousy" here to that of, say, teenage friendship or romance, it will appear petty and ridiculous. But if you compare it with the jealousy directed at the one who steals a spouse, or the cult that steals a child's loyalty, the impression changes. Jealousy can be holy and right. "His jealousy is not a moral flaw," writes respected theologian J. I. Packer, "but a moral excellence; it is the jealousy of a loyal husband who rightly desires his wife's exclusive affection" (*Keeping the Ten Commandments* [Crossway, 2008], 44). God's outrage at his people's infidelity through idol worship and the misuse of his name is not because he is a petulant bully—"a petty, unjust, unforgiving control-freak," as Richard Dawkins puts it (*The God Delusion*, 31)—but because he is the God and father of all. He cannot bear to watch us seduced and stolen away.

Personally, I want a Lord whose love is so great that he is moved to jealousy and outrage over my betrayal. And this is the context in which we are to understand the emotionally charged language that follows: "punishing the children for the sin of the parents to the third and fourth generation of those who hate me, but showing love to a thousand generations of those who love me and keep my commandments."

Three or four generations is what a healthy person in ancient times might hope to see in life: children by twenty years of age, grandchildren by forty, great grandchildren by sixty. That's four generations. (Most of us today only get to see *three* generations.) A thousand generations, on the other hand, is longer than all of recorded history. Even today, more than three millennia later, we are a mere 150 generations after Moses. The point appears to be that God's jealous outrage will be visible for the *totality* of the betrayer's life, whereas his blessing on the faithful will be beyond the human capacity to fathom.

This is one of those places where readers have to resist the urge to fret about the exact mathematics of God's judgment and blessing. It is true there are passages later in the Old Testament that make clear God will *not* punish children for the wrongdoing of parents (Ezekiel 18:1 – 20). But rushing to that text to neutralise this one seems insensitive to the purpose of the heightened language of the second commandment. Equally inappropriate, in my view, is raising logistical hypotheticals about what happens to, say, the *third* generation of a guilty family if they repent of the sins of the first generation, or what happens to the 150th direct descendant of a faithful Israelite who then abandons Yahweh for a false god. This sort of thinking leads us astray. I think we are just meant to let the extremity of the language — genuine hyperbole — wash over us and have its effect. We are to stand in awe of the God who takes us so seriously, who loves us so passionately, that our betrayal moves him to outrage and our love moves him to such extravagance. In time the New Testament will declare that the heights of God's judgment and love are seen most clearly in the sacrificial death of Jesus Christ. There the severe punishment due to God's people fell upon God's own Son, so that all might be freely forgiven. But that is to get ahead of myself.

The other thing we must do in order to hear these warnings the way ancient Israel heard them is to recall the *logic* of taking God seriously in first place. God first took Israel seriously — set his love on them and saved them, as the opening words of God's *torah* make clear, "I am the LORD your God, who brought you out of Egypt, out of the land of slavery." No matter how strong is the call to obedience, no matter how fearsome is the threat of punishment, the basis of Israel's relationship with God is his prior work of salvation. He has proven the seriousness of his love for Israel. The first three commandments emphasise the seriousness with which Israelites (and all who stand in their tradition) were to take up the name of God on their lips.

Followers of Jesus have appreciated this point just as keenly as the students of Moses. After all, Christians claim that God has done more than reveal his name. He has shown up with a face and given himself for us on a cross. I know many readers won't share that perspective, but that's what Christianity proclaims. And now Christians go by his name: they are "Christ"-ians. God's *new* covenant, in other words, calls not for less seriousness than the old covenant, but more.

In my *Life of Jesus* (Zondervan, 2010) I told a story about a young deserter in the army of Alexander the Great — I have not been able to verify it, because I don't want to know if it's untrue! But it illustrates my point well. As Alexander moved eastward—through Persia toward India—conditions became tough and soldiers began to desert. Typically, such cowards were shown no mercy. They would be hunted down by Alexander's loyal guard and killed. A story is told of an exception. A young man had secretly left the camp in search of freedom and comfort. He was promptly found and brought back to the king. It must have been a terrifying experience to stand guilty in the presence of the most powerful man on earth. For reasons unknown Alexander apparently decided to let the man go unpunished, but not before asking his name. "My name is Alexander, my King, just like yours," said the deserter. The battle-weary monarch replied in words that I can only imagine left an impression. "Young man, change your life or change your name!"

In just about every way, Alexander and Jesus were different leaders. The one conquered nations with unprecedented might, the other with sacrificial love. But there is a truth in Alexander's words that every follower of Christ recognizes. To call oneself a "Christian" is to hold the name of the greater king, Christ. And it ought to change life.

My point is that biblical faith—taking up the name of the Lord—should never be a trivial, commercial, or deceitful thing. It is serious business. No doubt some readers have encountered examples of hypocritical religion that have tarnished the reputation of the church irreparably. All I can say is that the Ten Commandments and the teaching of Jesus demand something different. For his own honour and for the welfare of all, God demands that those who take up his name on their lips do so honestly and sincerely.

7

WORK, PLAY, AND WORSHIP: *FOURTH COMMANDMENT*

In the fourth commandment we find a little relief from the seriousness of the first three. In fact, it is all about relief, or rest from work. If you're someone who enjoys a weekend, you owe it to Moses:

> Six days you shall labor and do all your work, but the seventh day is a sabbath to the LORD your God. On it you shall not do any work, neither you, nor your son or daughter, nor your male or female servant, nor your animals, nor any foreigner residing in your towns. For in six days the LORD made the heavens and the earth, the sea, and all that is in them, but he rested on the seventh day. Therefore the LORD blessed the Sabbath day and made it holy. (Exodus 20:9 – 11; see also Deuteronomy 5:12 – 15)

THE MYSTERIOUS ORIGINS OF THE SABBATH

The Sabbath day of rest is a historical mystery. After decades of searching, specialists have been unable to find any precedent or parallel that might have prompted the ancient Jews to propose a day off every seven days. There were days in pagan calendars when some forms of work were forbidden. Hesiod, one of the earliest known Greek writers (700 BC), tells us that no one should sow seed on the thirteenth day of a moon cycle, or plant crops on the sixteenth day, and so on. Legal business was also forbidden on certain days in the Greco-Roman world. These were all considered "unlucky" days and were associated with lunar movements. They had nothing to do with promoting rest and recuperation. As much as it galls some historians to concede, it really does look like those ancient Jews invented the tradition of a weekend off for all. (For the theologically minded, I should of course say that *God* invented it.) The authoritative *Anchor Bible Dictionary* acknowledges:

> In spite of the extensive efforts of more than a century of study into extra-Israelite sabbath origins, it is still shrouded in mystery. No hypothesis commands the respect of a scholarly consensus. Each hypothesis or combination of hypotheses has insurmountable problems. The quest for the origin of the sabbath outside of the OT [Old Testament] cannot be pronounced to have been successful. (*ABD* 5:851)

Wherever the Sabbath day of rest came from, it seems to have caught on. By at least the first century AD, more than a millennium after Moses, some Greeks and Romans had borrowed aspects of the Jewish day off. An aristocratic Jewish resident of Rome in the late first century wrote:

> The masses have long since shown a keen desire to adopt our religious observances; and there is not one city, Greek or barbarian, nor a single nation, to which our custom of

abstaining from work on the seventh day has not spread. (Josephus, *Against Apion* 2.282)

Josephus is exaggerating. Plenty of nations and cities ignored Jewish customs. But there is something in what he says. People were adopting the Jewish custom in Greco-Roman times. This only increased with the rise of Christianity.

A DOUBLE CORRECTIVE

As hard as it is for many Westerners to understand, weekly scheduled *rest* was a novelty in the ancient world. For most of history, the elites of a society tended to work as little as they possibly could, and the peasants worked pretty much all the time, week in, week out. The Sabbath command corrects both pagan traditions.

On the one hand, the fourth commandment strongly endorses *work*: "Six days you shall labor and do all your work." This is phrased like a command. Work is strongly affirmed. Jews took labour and output very seriously. Elites and peasants were both expected to live productive lives. In the biblical perspective, work is not a "necessary evil." It was part of the blessing of being a creature in God's good world. In the garden of Eden *before the "fall" into sin* Adam was productive: "The LORD God took the man and put him in the Garden of Eden to work it and take care of it" (Genesis 2:15).

Productive work is part of the blessing of creation. And so the fourth commandment begins with a reminder of its importance. The idea of not contributing in some way to the productivity of the world is very far from the Bible's idea of the Good Life. The goal to "retire by 50" is quite contrary to the Jewish and Christian Scriptures, which celebrate work as part of our purpose as human beings. The strong correlation between unemployment and depression today will be partly explained by loss of income and partly by the loss of a sense of usefulness (see the 2013 Gallup poll: http://www.gallup.com/poll/171044/depression-rates-higher-among-long-term-unemployed.aspx).

The main point of the Sabbath command, however, is to urge *rest* from work: the word *sabbath* itself comes from the verb "to cease, rest." The instruction offers a corrective to overwork. You honour God not only by working but also by resting. The fourth commandment—in the version in Exodus, anyway—drives this home by pointing back to the creation story itself: "in six days the LORD made the heavens and the earth, the sea, and all that is in them, but he rested on the seventh day." Leaving aside the thorny question of six-day creationism, discussed at length in my *Doubter's Guide to the Bible*, these words appear to be added to provide a powerful rationale or motivation for adherence to the command: God himself *works* and *rests*, he *creates* and *enjoys*. (Deuteronomy gives a different rationale, as we will see in a moment.)

There is a curious twin purpose of Sabbath rest. It honours God and benefits humankind (the twin purposes of the whole *torah*). Moses emphasises that "the seventh day is a Sabbath *to the LORD your God.*" The day of rest is meant to have a Godward dimension. In the course of history,

Jews have expressed this by making the Sabbath—which runs from Friday sunset to Saturday sunset—a day of study and prayer. I guess the Christian parallel is Sunday church attendance.

But there is also a "humanitarian impetus for such an institution," says Old Testament expert Carol Meyers (*Exodus* [Cambridge University Press, 2005], 132). Sabbath is about *us*. It mandates rest for workers. And notice that *all* are to rest. This is not just for elites and landholders. It is for sons and daughters, male and female servants, foreigners, and even animals.

The version of the Ten Commandments in Deuteronomy seems to lay stress on the humanitarian purpose of the Sabbath. All are forbidden to work, "*so that* your male and female servants may rest, as you do." Sabbath is a gift to humanity, just as much as it is a duty. There is a sense in which all of the Ten Commandments are intended for our good: living God's way puts us in harmony with his world and with his purposes for our lives. It is following the "manufacturer's instructions." But the fourth commandment seems especially designed for our tangible benefit.

SABBATH IN THE NEW TESTAMENT

Jesus laid stress on this *humanitarian* purpose of the Sabbath when he, or his band of disciples, was accused of breaking the fourth commandment. His entourage had picked some grain in a field on a Saturday. According to the strict interpretation of *torah* offered by the Pharisees (a devout renewal movement in Jesus's day), this constituted *farm work*:

The Pharisees said to him, "Look, why are they doing what is unlawful on the Sabbath?"...Then he said to them, "The Sabbath was made for man, not man for the Sabbath. So the Son of Man is Lord even of the Sabbath." (Mark 2:24, 27–28)

There has always been a spectrum of views on what constitutes "work" on the Sabbath. Not everyone in Jesus's day believed picking grain heads broke the fourth commandment, just as not every Jew today follows the Orthodox practice in Israel of not pressing the button of a hotel lift on the Sabbath (non-Jewish travellers to Israel are amazed to find lifts that automatically go to every floor between Friday sundown and Saturday sundown).

It is fascinating that Jesus did not criticise the Pharisees for having too strict a definition of work. Instead, he says they have missed the very point of the Sabbath. For him, the fourth commandment is not so much about humanity's obligation to God, but God's good gift to humanity: "The Sabbath was made for man, not man for the Sabbath." Rest from work was never meant to be another weight around our neck. It was a divine provision for those already weighed down by the toils of the world. That was Jesus's perspective, and it shaped ours.

This reframing of the Sabbath—which is already present in the fourth commandment itself—sets the trajectory for the relaxed approach (no pun intended) of the New Testament toward Sabbath-keeping.

There are numerous hints in the New Testament that the first believers generally kept the Jewish Sabbath. The first Christians were all Jews, after all. The disciples rested on the

Saturday between Jesus's crucifixion and the discovery of the empty tomb (Luke 23:56). A certain distance within the suburbs of Jerusalem is described as a "Sabbath day's walk," a reference to the short travel distance permissible on the Jewish day of rest (Acts 1:12). And the apostle Paul affirms the Jewish believer who "considers one day more sacred than another" (Romans 14:5).

But there is another story. At least two passages make clear that Christians were not to judge one another if they chose *not* to keep a complete day of rest. While it is true in the passage just mentioned that Paul defends the believer who regards one day more sacred — a reference to the Jewish Sabbath — he equally defends the one who doesn't: "One person considers one day more sacred than another; another considers every day alike. Each of them should be fully convinced in their own mind" (Romans 14:5).

In another context, Paul explicitly forbids anyone looking down on another over Sabbath-keeping:

> Therefore do not let anyone judge you by what you eat or drink [a reference to Jewish food laws], or with regard to a religious festival, a New Moon celebration or a Sabbath day. These are a shadow of the things that were to come; the reality, however, is found in Christ. (Colossians 2:16–17)

Sabbath is not a duty hanging over us or a moral principle allowing us to judge others. It is God's wise gift to us.

Particularly interesting is the way Paul describes the Sabbath — and other elements of the Jewish *torah* — as "a shadow of the things that were to come; the reality, however, is found in Christ." The Sabbath points forward to something, and this introduces the final biblical thing I want to say about the Sabbath.

SABBATH IS A SIGN OF SALVATION

I mentioned earlier that the version of the fourth commandment we find in Deuteronomy offers a different rationale for enjoying rest: not that God himself works and rests (as in Exodus 20) but that God has saved his people from slavery in Egypt. Here is Moses's second rendition of the command:

> Remember that you were slaves in Egypt and that the LORD your God brought you out of there with a mighty hand and an outstretched arm. *Therefore* the LORD your God has commanded you to observe the Sabbath day. (Deuteronomy 5:15)

In this version of the commandment, rest from work seems to function as a picture of salvation, a token of divine grace. Leaving the toil of the working week for a period of joyful relaxation provides a weekly reminder of God's deliverance from hardship. This, too, is a theme that comes into special focus in the New Testament. In a complex passage in the book of Hebrews—a text all about how the new covenant fulfils the old—the writer describes Israel's deliverance from Egypt and entry into the Promised Land as a "Sabbath rest." He then compares this Sabbath with the ultimate Sabbath of entering God's kingdom:

> Therefore, since the promise of entering his rest still stands, let us be careful that none of you be found to have

fallen short of it. For we also have had the good news proclaimed to us, just as they did; but the message they heard was of no value to them, because they did not share the faith of those who obeyed. Now we who have believed enter that rest....There remains, then, a Sabbath-rest for the people of God; for anyone who enters God's rest also rests from their works, just as God did from his. Let us, therefore, make every effort to enter that rest. (Hebrews 4:1–3, 9–11)

As I say, the passage is complicated. But all I want us to observe is that "Sabbath" is a picture of resting in God's salvation—whether the salvation of ancient Israel or the salvation promised by Jesus Christ. This is an extension—a "refraction"—of the logic of the fourth commandment as it appears in Deuteronomy: keep a weekly Sabbath because the Lord has rescued you. Sabbath is a sign of salvation.

WORK, REST, AND FAITH

The Western world has been shaped by the Jewish perspective on work and rest. Work is not a necessary evil—a way of paying the bills. It is holy in itself. Tending the "garden" of the world, as Genesis puts it, is part of our purpose as creatures made in the image of God. Even in retirement, finding a way to contribute to the world's productivity will be satisfying, assuming it is matched to capacities. The idea of working for forty years, then "checking out" and going to the beach is not really our calling. Even those who can't get work, or who don't need to work, are still "wired" to live productive lives in the home, or in the community, or in the church. This is how Western society has viewed these things for centuries, but it certainly didn't come from Greece or Rome.

This Judeo-Christian work ethic has also always been balanced with a healthy approach to *rest*, for both elites and the poor, wherever possible. With the conversion of the Roman Empire to Christianity during the second to fourth centuries, our notion of a mandated civic day off—based on the Jewish model—was introduced by Emperor Constantine in a law of AD 321. It forbade all work for townsfolk (farmers could labour as they thought necessary). It must have been a joyful moment in Roman history, as the age-old patterns of *rest for elites* and *work for peasants* were overthrown, for good. As I say, we owe our weekend to Moses and Jesus. If we are not taking regular rest, we are robbing ourselves and our families of one of God's precious gifts. Or for those who prefer a less theological way of putting it, we are robbing ourselves of one of the healthiest gifts the Bible has granted to Western culture.

I was recently in South Korea where the tradition of *all-work-no-rest* looms large. It starts young. Many students go to evening as well as day classes, run either by the school or by one of the 25,000 *hagwons*, private out-of-hours institutions designed to give students an edge. Fourteen-hour school days is the norm for many Koreans. I was delighted to be at a conference in Korea for Christian teachers from around Asia. Since the 1970s, Christianity in Korea (and elsewhere in Asia) has grown exponentially, with almost a third of the country now claiming Christian faith. I heard about one Christian school in the country where the leadership refused to offer evening lessons and strongly urged students and their parents not to attend *hagwons*. It was quite a challenge to the surrounding culture, where the Confucian work ethic has reigned for centuries. It was also a potential risk to the competitive advantage of the school. But a few years into the innovation, I am told this school is one of the leading academic institutions in the region. The school officials I spoke to put it down to the biblical model: work *and rest*. As Christianity continues to influence Korean politics I can only hope that other examples of the Judeo-Christian work-and-rest ethic take hold. I was interested to read recently that South Korea has the fastest *declining* working times of all 36 OECD countries, from 2512 hours per year per worker in the year 2000 (which was the highest in the OECD at the time) to 2163 hours in 2012 (http://stats.oecd.org/Index.aspx?DatasetCode=ANHRS). That might not sound like much, but if those 349 *unworked* hours each year are being spent on rest, I am sure Korean families are feeling the difference. I don't know if the reported efforts of the Korean government to bring down the working hours of its citizens are the result of any Christian influence, but it is exactly the sort of thing the Judeo-Christian worldview ought to inspire. On this score at least, Australians look thoroughly "Christian," with 477 more unworked hours up the sleeve than their Korean counterparts, the equivalent of nearly sixty eight-hour days!

In all seriousness, busyness culture is sub-Christian. It is one of the West's increasing departures from its own cultural heritage. I don't just mean that in recent decades shops no longer close on Sundays. That's just a token of a larger abandonment of the discipline of rest (rest, like work, requires discipline). Many of us now applaud busyness, so much so that the appropriate response to the question, "How are you going?" now seems to be "Busy!" followed an approving chorus of "Hmms" and "I know what you mean." I reckon the Creator winces every time we do it—not just at the busyness itself, but at the way we are programmed to prize relentless busyness almost as a virtue.

I am also sure that busyness can cripple spiritual faith, just as rest can nourish it. The fourth commandment speaks of keeping the Sabbath "to the LORD." It says Sabbath is a sign of salvation. If we do not create sufficient space in our lives for reflecting on the big things, it shouldn't surprise us that we experience a narrowing of the spiritual field. I know for myself that when I am all *go go go*, racing from one thing to another, filling every moment with appointments and meetings, taking calls, texting, Facebooking, and so on, I have little headspace for God. And I am a professional God-botherer!

I remember an entire season of my career when this was so. In the late 1990s I worked half-time for one church and half-time as a consultant for sixty-five Anglican churches on the North Shore of Sydney. I worked full days, was out five nights a week, and I was completing my PhD in the wee hours of each morning. None of this is remarkable, but I sure learnt a lesson. Not only was this pace detrimental to my health, family, and friendships, it was a hazard to my Christian faith. Here I was "working for God" and yet resenting pretty much all of it. Prayer and reflection suffered. I felt like a hypocrite. I was.

Perhaps this only has special resonance with my devout or "professionally Christian" readers. But my intended point is broader: If *Christian* busyness can damage faith, any kind of busyness can diminish our spiritual perspective. I believe God has built us for productivity and gifted us with rest. And that rest — the sign of salvation — can be a key to knowing and sensing divine grace. There is therefore a logical connection between the first three commandments and the fourth commandment. The demand to take God seriously is followed by a call to give space in your life, in body and soul, to ponder the goodness and greatness of the Creator.

8
FAMILY MATTERS: *FIFTH COMMANDMENT*

With the fifth commandment we move from Godward duties to humanward ones. It isn't surprising that the first such command concerns the most profound and influential of all human ties—children to their parents:

> Honour your father and your mother, so that you may live long in the land the LORD your God is giving you. (Exodus 20:12; Deuteronomy 5:16)

The command is straightforward, but the implications have been far-reaching for Western ethics, and continue to be so.

THE MYTH OF THE "NUCLEAR FAMILY"

I was recently interviewed for Australia's ABC Radio National on the fraught topics of marriage and family. I imagine I was the token (semi-)conservative. The other guest was the immensely articulate Gene Robinson, the celebrated marriage equality campaigner and the first openly gay bishop of the Episcopal (or Anglican) Church of America. Part of his case for a new approach to marriage and family, made in the interview and in his publications, is the claim that the contemporary notion of the "family" is itself new and hardly known in biblical times:

> We must be very careful not to project our current understanding of marriage and "family values" back onto an ancient time, when such notions would have been foreign to that culture. It must be noted that the model of family we have today—that is, the so-called nuclear family—would have been unknown in ancient times, when the extended family was the norm. Married couples often lived in a household with parents, children, and other relatives. People were much less mobile than today, and families lived, worked, and socialized as extended family units. One man married to one woman, living in a home with only their children, was a rarity. (Gene Robinson, *God Believes in Love: Straight Talk about Gay Marriage* [Knopf, 2012], 116)

Robinson's point is that the modern world is too fixated on a model of family that is itself a recent creation. If the notion of "one man married to one woman, living in a home with only their children" is a cultural relativity, then we should be more open to other renditions of "family," including where one man is married to another man, living in a home with (or without) children, and so on.

Without touching on the broader issue of same-sex relationships, Robinson is wide of the mark in his description of the historical family. He is right that critics of same-sex relationships need to be careful they don't impose modern ideas onto biblical texts, but, equally, gay rights activists need to avoid the temptation to project their hypothetical ideals onto the historical record. There is a truth in what Robinson says, but it hides a significant falsehood.

Throughout history, as in the Bible, the prized norm of society has indeed been the "nuclear family." It is true that these families were far more connected to other families than our highly mobile culture today allows, but no one back then imagined that the basic family unit was anything other than one man married to one woman, living in a home with their children. Ancient life was village life. This meant that new families often lived next door to their parents or their brothers and sisters. We find evidence in towns such as Capernaum, Jesus's home base in Galilee, of families living in small, individual dwellings around a shared courtyard. This proximity to relatives meant that the nuclear family sat within a lovely, wider web of relationships—similar to life in many rural settings today—but this did not affect the ancient perspective of what constituted the fundamental family unit: parents with their children.

The norm of family life in the Bible is captured in that founding statement of Genesis, which still makes an appearance in traditional wedding services: "a man leaves his father and mother and is united to his wife, and they become one flesh" (Genesis 2:24). Thus begins a new division in the family unit. The same is true, incidentally, of the ancient Roman family. "The evidence of epitaphs illustrates close family ties," says the entry on "Family" in the authoritative *Oxford Classical Dictionary*. "Although ties with remoter relations by blood or marriage are acknowledged when they exist, emphasis is normally on the nuclear family, one's wife/husband and children, or parents and siblings" (Simon Hornblower, ed., *The Oxford Classical Dictionary* [Oxford University Press, 2003], 586). The nuclear family is not a modern invention.

The Ten Commandments offer a snapshot of the ancient version of family—the nuclear family—that has shaped the Western world. The fifth commandment itself concerns parents and their children. But the seventh commandment concerns a husband and his wife ("do not commit adultery"). This is the ideal of the "family" contemplated in the commandments: a husband faithful to his wife and children honouring their parents.

Not for a moment do I want to diminish other forms of family life that exist today—single parent families, spouses without children, and so on. It is right that "traditionalists" (like me) are challenged by the needs and concerns of those who walk another path. Here, I am just trying to set the historical record straight, lest the nuclear family itself be viewed with disdain as a mere cultural quirk of modernity (someone recently criticised my current Facebook profile picture of my family as "So hetero-normative, an attempt to project the values of heterosexuality and procreation typical of the Christian Right." Yikes!). The reality is, for at least three thousand years the prized basic unit of settled society has been *one man married to one woman, living in a home with their children*. I don't believe every family has to look like this in order for society to survive and thrive, but I do believe a culture diminishes itself where this model is not a celebrated norm.

TO REGARD AS *HEAVY*

Even closer than marital ties, the connection between parents and children heads the Ten Commandments' vision of the Good in human relationships. Parents are the bridge between our Godward duties and our humanward ones. This is an observation made in the oldest interpretation of the Ten Commandments we possess, that of the Jewish intellectual Philo of Alexandria (early first century AD), who writes:

> For parents themselves are something between divine and human nature, partaking of both; of human nature, inasmuch as it is plain that they have been born and that they will die; and of divine nature, because they have engendered other beings, and have brought what did not exist into existence: for, in my opinion, what God is to the world, that parents are to their children. (Philo, *Special Laws* 2.225)

The point is not merely poetic. There is something structurally equivalent between the reverence due to the Maker and the honour due to a mother and father. After all, under normal conditions parents are our first source, carer, protector, teacher, benefactor, and so on. They are godlike.

The fifth commandment stresses the importance of the child-parent relationship by using a *weighty* term. The word "honour" in "*Honour* your father and your mother" is the Hebrew verb *kaved*, meaning "to be heavy." We are to consider our parents "weighty." We echo a similar notion when we describe a serious conversation with a friend as "heavy" or "weighty" or when we describe a leader as having *gravitas*, which derives from the Latin for "heavy." *Kaved* is frequently used of "giving glory" to God himself (Isaiah 24:15; Psalm 22:24). The fifth commandment calls for more than simply obeying parents or speaking nicely of them. It asks children (dependent children or adult children) to adopt a stance toward their parents that pays them deep—almost divine—respect.

Attached to the fifth commandment is a promise that underlines the weightiness of the relationship between children and parents: "so that you may live long in the land the LORD your God is giving you." I said in chapter 3 that this particular promise of blessing has a direct relevance only to Israel living in the Promised Land. The covenant God made with the Israelites had certain blessings (and curses) that did not have universal application. In other words, it would be wrong to think the fifth commandment is promising flourishing crops, or increased stocks, for those who honour parents. Rightly understood, the Bible does not teach a "prosperity gospel."

That said, I also pointed out in chapter 3, there is *some* ongoing relevance to this promise of blessing. In the New Testament Paul happily quotes the fifth commandment to his Ephesian audience—who were neither Jews nor living in the land of Israel—and he makes a point of calling it "the first commandment with a promise" and then cites the words "so that it might go well with you" (Ephesians 6:3). The logic of blessing attached to this commandment, in other words, runs deeper than the specific situation of the Israelites in their land. And it is not hard to imagine why. As the fundamental unit of society, the nuclear family is the first source of human flourishing for all communities. Again, I realise there are many different kinds of family in the modern world, and I don't want to suggest they are somehow inherently less valuable than nuclear families. They are not. Yet, I find it hard to deny that the relationship of children to their parents is society's great engine of boundless good (and therefore also potentially, of course, of tragic harm). It makes sense in this context that the fifth commandment would head the list of our humanward duties and that it would be the only commandment with the explicit promise, "that it might go well with you." *Family* is the weightiest of matters.

OBEDIENCE OF DEPENDENTS

When children are dependents, honouring parents naturally entails *obeying* them, as the Old Testament itself remarks (Deuteronomy 21:18). The New Testament echoes the sentiment unchanged. The apostle Paul, as I have just said, quotes the fifth commandment intact when directly addressing children in the church of Ephesus:

> Children, obey your parents in the Lord, for this is right. "Honour your father and mother"—which is the first commandment with a promise—"so that it may go well with you and that you may enjoy long life on the earth." (Ephesians 6:1–2)

It must be said that there are clearly limits to a child's obligation to obey parents, such as when a parent demands something illegal or harmful for the child. But it is too easy, under normal circumstances, for dependents to find reasons not to obey parents. Our culture sometimes encourages disobedience of parents by making it appear daring and cool (I feel decidedly middle-aged even writing this, but I still think it's worth noting!).

I know from experience that there are sometimes even "pious" motivations for disobedience. In my early zeal as a new teenage Christian I frequently found ways to elevate my "faith" above my duties to my mother (I lost my father years earlier). I remember one Saturday morning kneeling by my bed reading my Bible and praying. A voice came from the other end of the house, "John, it's your turn to rake the leaves on the front lawn!" I yelled back with all sincerity, "I can't right now. I'm in the middle of something really important!" The instruction grew louder and my reply more earnest. A few minutes later my mother burst into the room to repeat her command, and there she found me in all my *faux* piety. Disgusted, she walked right back out of the room. It pains me to admit it now, but in that moment I thought I was being "persecuted," just like the ancient Christians! It is an embarrassing memory, especially as there was no reason I couldn't pray *while raking the leaves*.

THE SUPPORT OF ADULT CHILDREN

There comes a point when honouring parents no longer means obedience, but support. As I have said already, the Bible teaches that marriage establishes a new core family unit:

Then the LORD God made a woman from the rib he had taken out of the man, and he brought her to the man. The man said, "This is now bone of my bones and flesh of my flesh; she shall be called 'woman,' for she was taken out of man." That is why *a man leaves his father and mother* and is united to his wife, and they become one flesh. (Genesis 2:22–24)

In marriage there is a conceptual "leaving" of parents. And this was the case even when the newlyweds moved just next door or across the courtyard. In a very real sense, children one day *leave* their parents to *cleave* to another person (if this were a different kind of book, we might explore the problems that arise when parents don't let their married children emotionally leave!). This leaving and cleaving does not negate the command to "Honour your father and mother." The Ten Commandments were addressed to adult Israelites as much as their children. Yet this new situation does reframe the fifth commandment.

To "honour" parents once you have left home means to *support* them. This is precisely how Jesus read the fifth commandment, and his interpretation greatly impacted early Christianity and, in the course of time, Western culture. In criticizing the Pharisee wing of first-century Judaism, he said:

"You have a fine way of setting aside the commands of God in order to observe your own traditions! For Moses said, 'Honour your father and mother,' and, 'Anyone who curses their father or mother is to be put to death.' But you say that if anyone declares that what might have been used to help their father or mother is Corban (that is, devoted to God) — then you no longer let them do anything for their father or mother. Thus you nullify the word of God by your tradition that you have handed down. And you do many things like that." (Mark 7:9–13)

The Pharisees had developed an elaborate system of additional commands. They had counted up the 613 instructions of the Old Testament and then devised literally thousands of related commands designed to make it harder to break one of the original laws. In Jesus's day these extra commandments were a vast *oral* tradition, passed on from teacher to student. They were eventually codified and written down by the great scholar-rabbi Judah the Prince around the year AD 200 in the Galilean town of Sepphoris, just a short walk from the satellite village of Nazareth. The written collection of these oral laws is known as the Mishnah (from the word for "repetition"), and it remains sacred literature for Orthodox Jews to this day. We don't find an exact parallel in the Mishnah to the law criticized above by Jesus — perhaps the Pharisees thought better of the idea by AD 200 — but we do find evidence that *gifting goods to heaven* (*corban*) removed any claim others might have on them and, further, that personal vows had the power to ban others, including parents, from deriving a benefit from a son's property (Mishnah, *Nedarim* 5:6). Jesus confronted a version of this tradition that withheld material benefits for parents by technically gifting goods to God. Jesus condemned the practice as a breach of the fifth commandment. In doing so, he underlines his own understanding of the force of the commandment for adult children. The command to *honour one's father and mother* involves an obligation to care for their material needs.

CARE FOR THE ELDERLY

Jesus's rendition of the fifth commandment shaped early Christian practice and eventually wider Western culture. Caring for elderly parents—yours and others—became a crucial ministry of the church in its first few centuries. Consider the instructions of the apostle Paul to his delegate in Ephesus, Timothy:

> Give proper recognition to those widows who are really in need. But if a widow has children or grandchildren, these should learn first of all to put their religion into practice by caring for their own family and so repaying their parents and grandparents, for this is pleasing to God....Give the people these instructions, so that no one may be open to blame. Anyone who does not provide for their relatives, and especially for their own household, has denied the faith and is worse than an unbeliever. (1 Timothy 5:3–4, 7–8)

Strong words: members of the church who don't care for their own parents (or grandparents) are worse than those who have no faith. Indeed, to overlook one's elderly relatives is to deny the faith altogether. Paul could hardly have made the point more emphatically. Just as young children are to *obey* parents, older children are to *support* parents. This is how they were to regard them as "weighty."

By the middle of the first century the church had already established an informal welfare system for elderly parents who didn't have family to look after them. The passage just quoted continues, "If any woman who is a believer has widows in her care, she should continue to help them and not let the church be burdened with them, so that the church can help those widows who are really in need" (1 Timothy 5:16). Yes, it was a Christian's duty to care for the "widows" (and presumably needy "widowers") in their own family, but when that care was not present, the church itself stepped in to provide material support. The command to honour one's own parents *morphs* into a broader call to care for the elderly generally.

In the two hundred years following the writing of the New Testament, churches developed these systems of care so that by the fourth century there was a full blown "order of widows," a group of needy older women who were themselves supported materially by the church but who also were active in dispensing church funded provisions to others (on this see Patricia Cox Miller, *Women in Early Christianity: Translations from Greek Texts* [Catholic University of America Press, 2005], 49–61). Along with food distribution, monetary collections, and church hostels, hospices and hospitals, such widows' programs are the true origin of the massive tradition of welfare we now take for granted in the West. None of it derived from Greco-Roman culture: it is well known that social care was conspicuous by its absence in ancient Greece and Rome. Nor did it arise in recent history, as part of Enlightenment virtues. The humanitarian tradition of the West is an entirely Judeo-Christian inheritance.

One, of course, does not need to be a Christian in order to appreciate the importance of social welfare, and in recent years many excellent non-religious charities have been established. What I am saying here is that even the most secular aid agency in the West today finds its intellectual roots in the innumerable Christian charitable orders of late antiquity and, ultimately, in the explicit teaching of Moses, Jesus, and the apostles in the ancient and classical periods.

On the origins of charity in the Greco-Roman and Christian periods see the still classic, Arthur Robinson Hands, *Charities and Social Aid in Greece and Rome* (Cornell University Press, 1968). A very important recent volume is by Peter Brown, *Through the Eye of a Needle: Wealth, the Fall of Rome, and the Making of Christianity in the West, 350–550 AD* (Princeton University Press, 2012).

BOOK NOTES

AN AGING POPULATION

Care for the elderly will continue to be a major ministry of the church, and society, going forward. We are getting older, if you hadn't noticed. In the United States, for instance, the median age increased from 35.3 in 2000 to 37.2 in 2010 (US 2010 Census). That might not sound like much, but it has huge social significance. By 2030 19 percent of the US population will be 65 years or older, according to the US Administration on Aging. And those aged 85 years and older could grow from 5.5 million in 2010 to 19 million by 2050, or nearly 1 in 20 (US Census Bureau). By 2050, the number of the US population 65 years and older with Alzheimer's disease may triple from 5 million to as many as 16 million (US Alzheimer's Association). The Australian Bureau of Statistics is predicting almost identical developments for my country.

1. median age: 2010 Census figures: https://www.census .gov/newsroom/releases/archives/2010_census/cb11-cn147.html

2. 65+: http://www.aoa.acl.gov/Aging_Statistics/index.aspx

3. 85+: http://www.agingstats.gov/main_site/data/2012 _documents/population.aspx

4. dementia: https://www.alz.org/downloads/facts_figures _2012.pdf

For almost two thousand years the idea that all people are "weighty" has driven significant programs of care for orphans and widows—the two ends of the spectrum of the vulnerable. As I say, this is how we got our hospitals, orphanages, and aged care systems. And yet, just as the population is significantly *aging*, the beliefs that undergirded aged care through Western history are now waning. Of course, most of us love our mums and our grans. We don't need religion to tell us to look after them. But an instinctive connection to our own relatives will only get us so far. As more people move into high-care facilities and dementia units (often at a great distance from family members), society will need a solid intellectual grounding for increasing our contributions to those who no longer give anything back to society in the material sense.

Greece and Rome, as I say, had very little by way of philosophical reasoning that guaranteed the inherent "weightiness" of those who lacked social utility. So, at one end of life, infanticide was rife, frequently in the form of leaving unwanted infants on a rubbish dump, euphemistically known as *expositio*, "putting outside." At the other end of life, welfare for the aged and infirm was non-existent (outside of personal ties). Christianity changed all of that with its many programs for young and old. Indeed, after a couple of centuries of churches caring for abandoned infants, Christian influence led Rome itself, in a law of AD 374, to ban infanticide and make it, somewhat remarkably, the equivalent of *parricide* (the killing of a parent or relative). The church inherited from the Jews a theology of the gravity of all human beings, especially the vulnerable, and opened its doors to Jew and Gentile alike. And so was born the tradition of "charity" we now take for granted.

Educated Greeks and Romans criticized Christianity for all this. To them Christianity was a religion for the poor and useless. Centuries later, Friedrich Nietzsche echoed this perspective, heaping scorn on Christianity, in a quote offered earlier, as the "religion of pity that thwarts the law of evolution, preserving what is ripe for destruction and defending life's disinherited and condemned." My point is that as our population ages, as families become more mobile and more disconnected, as our society loses its acquaintance with the Judeo-Christian rationale that established and sustained the tradition of care for the vulnerable, the sentiment "everyone loves their gran" isn't going to sustain us. We need a revival of the fifth commandment in its Christian rendition:

to regard all human beings, and especially parents and the elderly, as godlike.

A PERSONAL REFLECTION

Protecting the elderly in an aging society may seem a grandiose way to end the chapter. So let me conclude with a simple, more personal reflection.

As I was preparing material for this chapter, I realised how easy it is as an adult son to convey to a parent that they are not weighty. Happily, I live in the same city as my mother and see her quite often. We speak on the phone, too. But sometimes I am rushing from one thing to another, or perhaps just feeling the pressure of a deadline, and my mother will ring. I am ashamed to say I occasionally pick up the call with, "Mum, I can't really talk right now. I'm in the middle of something important." And as those words leave my lips, I can almost hear my teenage self mouthing the same thing decades earlier to avoid doing the chores! I am sure I sometimes give the impression to my very patient mother that she is an interruption, a mild annoyance. I know this must be true because in recent times she often begins with, "I'm sorry to phone you. I know you're busy. . . ."

My mother is no longer a parent to be obeyed. Nor in our situation is she ever likely to need my financial assistance! But there she is, at the head of the Bible's list of humanward duties, godlike, my original source, carer, protector, teacher, and benefactor. She is weighty. And so this author is writing to himself as much as to anyone else: "Honour your father and your mother."

9

CHERISH YOUR NEIGHBOUR:
SIXTH COMMANDMENT

The next four commandments (6–9) are the most self-explanatory. Do we really need to be told, "Do not murder"? They are also much, much briefer than the others. In fact, there are just eleven words in total in the Hebrew text of these four commands, less than any other *individual* commandment (except the first). The next four chapters will be correspondingly brief, before concluding in chapter 13 with the challenging and unique tenth commandment (which has fifteen words). But first, another analogy.

SHADOWS AND REALITIES

I have said repeatedly that the Ten Commandments shaped the Western world not in their own right but through the particular rendition of Moses's words offered by Jesus. We find in the New Testament a clear transposition of the *torah*, as Jesus lifts the key in which the original tune is played. In addition to this musical analogy, I offered the picture in chapter 3 of "refraction," of light passing through a prism and bending and separating the wavelengths into the full spectrum of colour. Some things are intensified: for example, the command against idolatry is extended to include greed. Others are transformed almost beyond recognition: for example, the Sabbath command is interpreted principally as a sign of salvation, not an absolute ban on working.

Another metaphor might help us conceptualise this transition from old covenant to new covenant, and will help open up the sixth to the ninth commandments. It is a picture offered within the New Testament itself, in a passage quoted in chapter 7 in connection with the Sabbath:

> Therefore do not let anyone judge you by what you eat or drink, or with regard to a religious festival, a New Moon celebration or a Sabbath day. These are a shadow of the things that were to come; the reality, however, is found in Christ. (Colossians 2:16–17)

Here the apostle Paul wants us to think of Old Testament regulations concerning food, festivals, and the Sabbath day as a "shadow" of a larger reality brought about by Jesus Christ. Picture a long shadow in the afternoon sun cast by a large statue — perhaps an image of Christ. The shadow is dependent on the statue and utterly consistent with it. But we can only discover the true form of the object by looking directly at it. And when we do, the shadow itself becomes clearer, more explicable. As I have said previously, the Old Testament itself leads us to expect something like this: it tells us to wait for a new Moses; it predicts a "new covenant" that will "not be like the covenant I made with their ancestors."

Such New Testament talk grates with my Jewish friends, and I understand why. Yet it is hard to avoid the impression that the Old Testament deliberately points beyond itself, like a shadow to a future reality. Perhaps the Christian claim to represent that reality isn't true, but something like the great transposition brought about by Jesus of Nazareth is expected within the Old Testament. And, either way, the project of this book would be unaffected. Whatever the truth or falsehood of Christianity's claims, we can confidently say, as a simple historical statement, that it was the specifically *Christian* rendering of Moses's law that spread throughout Western society. While the *shadow-reality* understanding of the Old and New Testaments may be believed only by Christians, the cultural effect of this interpretation touches every citizen of the Western world. And the four brief commandments discussed below provide clear examples.

MURDER AND THE IMAGE OF GOD

The sixth commandment, "You shall not murder" (Exodus 20:13; Deuteronomy 5:17), is not exactly revolutionary in the history of ethical reflection. "Refrain from killing" also appears in the Maxims of Delphi discussed in chapter 1 (though it is perhaps surprising that it is listed at number 51). The biblical command is so straightforward it requires only two words in Hebrew: the particle "not" and the second person verb "murder."

Perhaps the only necessary commentary is to point out that the word "murder" (*ratsach*) is not the more general term "kill" (*harag*). The sixth commandment does not proscribe the slaying of animals, killing in warfare, or the death penalty, all of which are endorsed, under certain constraints, in the Old Testament *torah*. The command refers to the deliberate and unlawful killing of one human being by another: murder.

The commandment itself is not unique, but the logic of the biblical injunction against murder is. To recall the discussion of chapter 2, if you were to ask a thoughtful atheist about murder, you would of course receive an unequivocal answer: murder is wrong. The grounds for such an absolute moral statement would probably include reference to the kind of society we want to live in. To countenance murder is to countenance a society without order, and so everyone suffers. Some atheists may instinctively want to go further and speak of the *sanctity of life* or the *inalienable rights* of every soul. Yet, as atheist philosopher Raimond Gaita rightly observes, such language is "problematic and contentious" without a religious framework. "These are ways of trying to say what we feel a need to say when we are estranged from the conceptual resources we need to say it" (Raimond Gaita, *Thinking about Love and Truth and Justice* [Routledge, 2002], 24). He specifically means that these are Judeo-Christian ways of talking about human obligations, and that without that religious framework—a state of affairs he would welcome—they are inappropriate for a mature secular society. New ethical justifications and language are required, even if the same ethical maxims are shared. Personally, I feel this is one of the most interesting features of thoughtful contemporary atheism: how to endorse the basic ethical norms granted to the West by centuries of biblical influence *without* holding any biblical beliefs about the world and humanity?

What is the biblical logic for the injunction against murder? Christian ethics is rarely predicated on a utilitarian model of *what is best for society* (even if the biblical path is thought to result in blessings for society). The obvious problem with this approach is: who gets to decide what's best for society? Some ancient cultures genuinely believed that human sacrifice fostered social stability. Others imagined that enforced domination of other peoples would establish universal peace: e.g., the *Pax Romana*. Biblical social ethics is less concerned with an (imagined) results approach, and more driven by a recognition of the high value of human beings. Every man and woman, regardless of capacity or utility, is *intended by God* to *bear his image* in the world.

One of the earliest references to murder in the Bible appeals to the high status of human beings: "Whoever sheds human blood, by humans shall their blood be shed; for in the image of God has God made mankind" (Genesis 9:6). We might see this as contradiction: if you murder, you will be murdered. But the reference here is to capital punishment. The Old Testament permits capital punishment as a *divinely sanctioned* judgment. That's the point: only God can sanction the death of those bearing his image. (Incidentally, I oppose the death penalty on theological and sociological grounds in this new covenant era.)

My point is that while all reasonable men and women will oppose murder, either instinctively or on utilitarian grounds, the Judeo-Christian worldview provides a powerful *additional* rationale that has informed ethical thinking for centuries. For those who see humanity as intended by God to bear his image, expressions such as "sanctity of life" and "inalienable rights" are not outmoded expressions. They are reflections of reality. "Human life is thus the most precious and sacred thing in the world," says the Canadian theologian J. I. Packer, "and to end it, or direct its ending, is God's prerogative alone. We honor God by respecting his image in each other, which means consistently preserving life and furthering each other's welfare in all possible ways" (*Keeping the Ten Commandments,* 78).

The high value placed on humanity in biblical logic means that the command "Do not murder" could never be read as permission to mistreat one's neighbour all the way up to, but not including, the premeditated taking of their life! The sixth commandment is a signpost to something more; as Packer says to "furthering each other's welfare." So it is not surprising that Jesus—the new Moses—would draw our attention from the shadow to the reality.

MURDER AND THE LAW OF LOVE

Early on in the Sermon on the Mount, Jesus cites the sixth commandment and gives the most extraordinary extrapolation of its intention:

> "You have heard that it was said to the people long ago, 'You shall not murder, and anyone who murders will be subject to judgment.' But I tell you that anyone who is angry with a brother or sister will be subject to judgment. Again, anyone who says to a brother or sister, 'Raca,' is answerable to the court. And anyone who says, 'You fool!'

will be in danger of the fire of hell. Therefore, if you are offering your gift at the altar and there remember that your brother or sister has something against you, leave your gift there in front of the altar. First go and be reconciled to them; then come and offer your gift." (Matthew 5:21–24)

Jesus employs hyperbole here. He often does. There's no way he was advocating taking cases of name-calling to "*the* court," especially as the word used here, *sunedriô*, refers to the high court or Sanhedrin of Israel, a legislative assembly of seventy-one aristocrats! The point is over the top, but no less clear. For Jesus, the command about murder is a shadow of a deeper reality in which God calls on us to revere people so much that we will refuse even to denigrate another: *raca* is an Aramaic insult emphasizing the *worthlessness* of someone ("good for nothing," "empty head"). More than that, we will value our neighbours so highly we will even suspend the worship of God to first make amends with a neighbour we have wronged (the expression "has something against you" refers to an objective harm you have caused your neighbour, not merely someone's displeasure with you).

I will never forget the Christian conference I attended years ago, when a large pious family moved into the row in front of me, and as they passed some teenagers sitting with their feet up on the nice theatre chairs, "Mrs. Christian" yelled at them, "We pay $100 each for those. Get your feet off!" As the young men left the building muttering obscenities, this family of believers placed their Bibles on their chairs, stood up, and raised their hands to join in the songs of praise now underway. It was an ugly counter example of the very thing Jesus emphasised: one cannot demean those made in God's image and then presume to worship God himself. Jesus's brother James in a later New Testament letter said much the same thing: "With the tongue we praise our Lord and Father, and with it we curse human beings, who have been made in God's likeness. Out of the same mouth come praise and cursing. My brothers and sisters, this should not be" (James 3:9–10). As I have said previously, the secular criticism of the religious hypocrite is not a secular criticism at all. It is thoroughly Christian.

The apostle John, an eyewitness to the life of Christ, a few decades after Jesus, connected the Old Testament injunction against murder to our neglect of the poor. Perhaps that sounds farfetched, but he was no doubt recalling Jesus's intensification of the sixth commandment: to demean another is to commit a murder of the heart. Therefore, to "hate" the poor by leaving them in their diminished state is to act like the first recorded murderer in the Bible, Cain:

> For this is the message you heard from the beginning: We should love one another. Do not be like Cain, who belonged to the evil one and murdered his brother.... Anyone who hates a brother or sister is a murderer, and you know that no murderer has eternal life residing in him. This is how we know what love is: Jesus Christ laid down his life for us. And we ought to lay down our lives for our brothers and sisters. If anyone has material possessions and sees a brother or sister in need but has no pity on them, how can the love of God be in that person? (1 John 3:11–12, 15–17)

This dazzling move from the command against "murder" to "pity" for the poor is premised on a simple logic. It is the rationale at the heart of all social ethics in the Bible. Human beings are loved and valued by the Creator. Not only are they made in God's image, they are creatures for whom Jesus Christ died. If that is true, a straight conceptual line can be drawn from murder to uncharitableness. Both are acts of demeaning what is inestimably precious. John Calvin, the sixteenth-century French reformer and theological genius, put it like this:

> If we do not wish to violate the image of God, we ought to hold our neighbor sacred. And if we do not wish to renounce all humanity, we ought to cherish his as our own flesh.... The Lord has willed that we consider those two things which are naturally in man, and might lead us to seek his preservation: to reverence his image imprinted in man, and to embrace our own flesh in him. He who has merely refrained from shedding blood has not therefore avoided the crime of murder. If you perpetrate anything by deed, if you plot anything by attempt, if you wish or plan anything contrary to the safety of a neighbor, you are considered guilty of murder. Again, unless you endeavor to look out for his safety according to your ability and opportunity, you are violating the law with a like heinousness. (*Institutes of the Christian Religion*, Book 2, 8.40)

I hardly need to point out that it is precisely this logic that lies behind the colossal tradition of charity that has characterized the West from the first century to today. I am thinking of the first-century widows' programs and the burgeoning food rosters of the third-century church. Then there are the empire-wide Christian hostels and aid programs mentioned even by the emperor (Julian) in the fourth century. By the ninth century, European monasteries were immense charitable institutions — almost cities — with accommodation, workshops, schools, and almshouses for the poor. Gratian's twelfth-century *Decretum*, a highly influential exposition of canon law, insisted that the rich were morally and legally obliged to assist the poor, a duty still felt by the most secular Western citizen (but not by people of the pre-Christian era). A century later we observe an astonishingly merciful approach to the "*poor* thief" in thirteenth-century church legal debate. No less part of this tradition are the spectacular human rights campaigns of the modern period. As Professor David Skeel of the University of Pennsylvania Law School has recently explained:

> The belief that each one of us is made in the image of God has been the inspiration for numerous human rights initiatives throughout history, including the efforts of the Early of Shaftesbury to improve the conditions of England's poor in the eighteen century and William Wilberforce's eventually successful quest to end England's slave trade in the nineteenth. In the twentieth century, this Christian belief served as the foundation for the United Nations Declaration of Human Rights, which was released in 1948 and is rightly seen as the start of the international human rights movement (although religious language was carefully omitted from it). (*True Paradox: How Christianity Makes Sense of our Complex World* [InterVarsity, 2014], 126–127)

And even today in Australia, eighteen of the twenty-five largest charities in the country are *Christian*. None of this came from Greece or Rome. It came from Moses and Jesus—the "shadow" and the "reality"—whether or not we believe we still need their help to nourish these traditions. Not for a moment am I suggesting that Christians are better than those without faith. In fact, I would happily acknowledge that secular humanitarians frequently put believers to shame with their commitment to justice and compassion. But I am saying—as a historical not theological claim—that both secular humanitarians and contemporary believers have inherited their way of thinking about the Good Life in large part from the specifically Judeo-Christian tradition of, as Calvin put it, "reverencing God's image imprinted in man."

10

HONOUR YOUR SPOUSE:
SEVENTH COMMANDMENT

The seventh commandment concerns sexual fidelity. Again, just two Hebrew words are required to make the point, translated into English, "You shall not commit adultery" (Exodus 20:14; Deuteronomy 5:18). Faithfulness to one's spouse, like the fifth commandment's call to honour parents, is at the heart of the biblical vision of human community. Israel knew that its society depended on the strength of the parent-child and the husband-wife relationship. The two are interrelated. The destruction of marriage through betrayal can devastate whole families, whole communities.

INFIDELITY TODAY

We often hear the statistic, "Half of all marriages end in divorce" and "Half of all married men are unfaithful." These are depressing figures. Although these statistics were probably invented — and it does seem they were invented — to scare people into faithfulness, some professionals worry that statements like these desensitize people to the tragedy of adultery. Some of us may even begin to think of it as inevitable and therefore defensible.

In a systematic review of research on infidelity, the *Journal of Marital and Family Therapy* reports that extramarital sex occurs in less than 25 percent of relationships. Moreover, it notes evidence that infidelity is significantly less common in *marriages* as opposed to *dating* or *cohabiting* relationships. Not only is infidelity in long term relationships less common than often imagined, it appears that *marriage* has a "commitment mechanism" that "may serve as a protective factor against infidelity" — though it is unclear whether marriage makes long-term couples more committed or whether more committed couples tend to get married (Adrian J. Blow and Kelley Hartnett, "Infidelity in Committed Relationships II: A Substantive Review," *JMFT* 31.2 [2005], 217–233). Of course, that adultery takes place in almost a quarter of marriages is alarming, but the fact that it does not occur in the significant majority of marriages is cause for admiration toward married couples.

Curiously, there is evidence across multiple studies that religious adherence reduces the likelihood of infidelity. This is *not* because religious folk are "better people" than non-religious. The same weaknesses and temptations are present in the church community as in the wider community. But nor is it simply a case of religious people falsely reporting their fidelity. Churches appear to provide external protective factors for marriage. The authors of the research review just mentioned propose several reasons why active religious affiliation has an effect on the likelihood of engaging in infidelity: religion's influence on relationship happiness generally, a religious person's more frequent exposure to messages critical of adultery, and, perhaps most significantly, "some of those who attend religious services have tighter social networks, and this exposure helps people to adhere to the norms of the community" (p. 223). In other words, if it is true that the seventh commandment is broken less often in religious circles, it has nothing to do with the internal goodness of individuals and much to do with the sociological effect of the biblical teaching itself and the kind of communities it tends to create. As I often say—mostly in jest—while believers cannot claim to be better people than non-believers, the ideals they hold are better. Put more simply, if you believe faithfulness to your spouse is one of the highest ideals you can attain to, you are less likely to commit adultery, especially if you are active in a community of people who share that ideal. If, on the other hand, you think fidelity is merely preferable but not vital, such a belief will no doubt influence how you respond to opportunities for sexual enjoyment with someone other than your spouse. Ideas matter. (Christians have additional reason for never thinking they are better human beings than anyone else: they believe that whatever ethical improvements they experience in life are the result of God's Spirit working within them. But that's a story for another kind of book entirely!)

SEX AND ONENESS

Perhaps the most powerful idea believers hold to is that every human being, regardless of capacity or utility, bears God's image and is so loved by him that Jesus Christ would "lay down his life for them," as the apostle John put it. This thought has implications not just for our approach to the safety of our neighbours (sixth commandment) but also for our approach to sex (seventh commandment).

In the Judeo-Christian tradition, sex has been seen as the sign and seal of the *self-giving of one human being to another*. More than pleasure, more than procreation, sex is sacred in the sense that it symbolises and achieves "oneness" between two individuals. The first reference to sex in the Bible emphasises this: "a man leaves his father and mother and is united to his wife, and they become one flesh" (Genesis 2:24). In the New Testament the apostle Paul likewise says that illicit sex still creates a kind of (illicit) oneness: "Do you not know that he who unites himself with a prostitute is one with her in body?" (1 Corinthians 6:16). Even the frequent euphemism for sex used throughout the Old Testament — to "know" a woman — is suggestive of this point. People sometimes make fun of the quaint terminology: "to *know* her, in the biblical sense!" But the Bible's choice of word isn't prudish (indeed, Scripture is frequently more open about sexual extravagance and deviance than polite secular society today). It underlines the intimacy-creating nature of intercourse. In an ideal setting, one comes to *know* a partner in a profound way through sexual intimacy. It's a point we can now also describe from a scientific perspective, as sexual health research stresses the "bonding hormones" released with sexual encounters. (See an interview on this question with Australian sex researcher, Dr. Patricia Weerakoon: https://publicchristianity.org/library/soul-sex-make-it-last-longer.)

The mental and spiritual dimensions of sex are stressed in Jesus's transposition of the seventh commandment. True to form, he takes the *torah* of Moses to a surprising level:

> "You have heard that it was said, 'You shall not commit adultery.' But I tell you that anyone who looks at a woman lustfully has already committed adultery with her in his heart." (Matthew 5:27–28)

There are two things to hold in mind before we can rightly feel the force of Jesus's remarks. First, the English adverb "lustfully" could imply that a mere feeling of arousal in the presence of another is wrong, is even adultery. But in the original Greek this is a *purpose clause* not an adverbial expression. It literally reads "Whoever looks at a woman *in order to lust* for her. . . ." The issue is not the feeling of arousal caused by looking at someone but rather the intention to look at someone in order to satisfy one's desire. The reference is to nursing desire, directing desire, aiming to fulfil desire. This is a kind of adultery, says Jesus.

The other thing to observe is that Jesus calls this a *kind of* adultery. It is adultery "in the heart," not actual adultery. It is similar to the way he described *anger* as "murder." The two are not strictly identical, as if he were of the opinion that someone should be locked up for being mean, or declared an adulterer for thoughts. The point is about the realities that underlie murder-hate and adultery-lust. For Jesus, the command against adultery is a shadow of a deeper reality in which God asks us to value the beloved—and sex itself—so highly that we will choose *not* to direct desire towards someone other than the one to whom we have pledged the "oneness" which sex is intended to embody.

THE VALUE OF SEX

It is precisely because the Bible has such a high view of the human person and of human sexuality that it has such seemingly limiting ideas about the appropriate context for sexual intimacy and even sexual thoughts. People sometimes slander the Bible as having too *low* a view of sex — as dirty and taboo. The opposite is the case. If I value my car, I will be careful how it is used and to whom I lend it. The Bible values sex enough to limit its enjoyment to the most intimate human relationship imaginable: one bound by the vow of lifelong commitment. A more secular, unrestrained approach might have the appearance of sexual "liberation" and "celebration" but it is frequently little more than a diminishing of sex's symbolic and relational power. It is lending out the car too freely! If you think of sex merely as a pleasurable physical experience, it probably makes sense to throw off any perceived shackles. So long as it's safe, it's fine. It is a bodily delight only, like eating an exquisite meal. But if you find yourself persuaded that sex is a joyous physical enactment of a profound spiritual truth about "oneness" with another human being, you will approach sexual activity very differently.

C. S. Lewis, the great Oxford literary don and public advocate of Christianity, once defended the biblical approach to sex against the call in his day (the 1940s) for more sexual "freedom." His insights are as relevant today as then:

I know some muddleheaded Christians have talked as if Christianity thought that sex, or the body, or pleasure, were bad in themselves. But they were wrong. Christianity is almost the only one of the great religions which thoroughly approves of the body—which believes that matter is good, that God himself once took on a human body, that some kind of body is going to be given to us even in heaven and is going to be an essential part of our happiness, our beauty and our energy. Christianity has glorified marriage more than any other religion: and nearly all the greatest love poetry in the world has been produced by Christians. If anyone says that sex, in itself, is bad, Christianity contradicts him at once... There is nothing to be ashamed of in enjoying your food: there would be everything to be ashamed of if half the world made food the main interest of their lives and spent their time looking at pictures of food and dribbling and smacking their lips. I do not say that you and I are individually responsible for the present situation. Our ancestors have handed over to us organisms which are warped in this respect: and we grow up surrounded by propaganda in favour of unchastity. There are people who want to keep our sex instinct inflamed in order to make money out of us. Because, of course, a man with an obsession is a man who has very little sales-resistance. God knows our situation; He will not judge us as if we had no difficulties to overcome. (C. S. Lewis, *Mere Christianity* [HarperCollins, 1997], 81–82)

I love Lewis's final, "pastoral" reflection for his audience: God mercifully takes our situation into account. Lewis knew that sexual sins are amongst the easiest and most guilt-inducing sins to commit (for many). He doesn't want to suggest that God is prudish and mean-spirited. He wants to reassure us that the biblical Lord tenderly allows us to approach him in all our weakness.

Lewis's words remind me of the other great reflection on the seventh commandment found in the life of Jesus. A woman is "caught in the act of adultery" (however that went down!) and is brought before him (John 8). The legal experts challenge his notoriously soft approach to sin. "In the Law Moses commanded us to stone such women," they reminded Jesus. "Now what do you say?" Jesus thought about it for a moment, and replied with those deservedly proverbial words, "Let any one of you who is without sin cast the first stone." As the accusers departed one by one, Jesus simultaneously comforted and challenged the woman: "neither do I condemn you. Go now and leave your life of sin" (John 8:11). While Jesus's understanding of the true demands of the seventh commandment was more intense than that of Moses, so was his assurance that God's first order of business is not condemnation but forgiveness.

11

GIVING WHAT IS DUE:
EIGHTH COMMANDMENT

Much of what I said earlier about murder applies also to the eighth commandment (and ninth). It concerns principles of justice toward others that arise from a high view of humanity. As a consequence, the command "You shall not steal" (Exodus 20:15; Deuteronomy 5:19) comes to refer to much more than theft.

The fundamental rationale of the eighth commandment is not so much the utilitarian aim of stable society, valuable as that is, but the inherent value of the neighbour made in God's image and loved by him. The more you value someone the less likely you are to take what is theirs against their will or without their knowledge.

I was a prolific shoplifter as a teenager. Usually it was just a bit of "hunting and gathering" in the local supermarket for my afternoon snack. But sometimes it was more. I was caught once, turned in by a friend. I was taken to the police station at North Sydney and, after a stern talking-to, I was placed in a cell with the door shut. It was designed to frighten me. It worked, but I didn't for a second let on.

Unfortunately, the experience did little to curb my teenage career in spurning the eighth commandment.

STEALING FROM THE POOR

In both Jewish and Christian tradition, stealing often meant much more than taking another's goods in a straightforward act of theft. In his famous exposition of the Ten Commandments, John Calvin in the sixteenth century enumerates the various forms of theft — violent robbery, fraud, and so on — before making the point that the inner meaning of the eighth commandment is a call never to deprive another of what is properly theirs. His wording may sound a little harsh or quaint to our ears, but the significance of Calvin's thought in these matters shouldn't be underestimated. He is one of the most influential thinkers — Christian or otherwise — in modern European history. Amid the linguistic oddities in the quotation below, I am sure you will hear something of the concerns that shape contemporary "secular ethical reasoning," including the important concept of a human "right":

> God sees the intricate deceptions with which a crafty man sets out to snare one of simpler mind, until he at last draws him into his nets. He sees the hard and inhumane laws with which the more powerful oppress and crush the weaker person. He sees the lures with which the wilier man baits, so to speak, his hooks to catch the unwary. All these things elude human judgment and are not recognized. And such injustice occurs not only in matters of money or in merchandise or land, but in the right of

each one; for we defraud our neighbors of their property if we repudiate the duties by which we are obligated to them.... [A]ll these are deemed theft in God's sight. For he who does not carry out what he owes to others according to the responsibility of his own calling both withholds and appropriates what is another's. We will duly obey this commandment, then, if, content with our lot, we are zealous to make only honest and lawful gain; if we do not seek to become wealthy through injustice, nor attempt to deprive our neighbour of his goods to increase our own.... And not this alone: but let us share the necessity of those whom we see pressed by the difficulty of affairs, assisting them in their need with our abundance. (John Calvin, *Institutes of the Christian Religion,* Book 2, 8.45.)

I am no fan of Calvin's ambitious project to establish a genuinely just and compassionate "Christian society" in the city of Geneva, but I can applaud his ethical aspirations. He was no moralist. He was a sophisticated social and theological thinker—and one of Geneva's best-trained lawyers—and he longed to see human communities flourish under the wisdom of God. Parts of early modern Europe were heavily influenced by him, as indeed all of Europe had been influenced by countless other important religious thinkers before him.

The connection between stealing and mistreating the poor was not an imaginative flourish of Calvin. Hints of it are found in both the Old and New Testaments, and these contributed to the development of the tradition of welfare in the ancient and medieval West described earlier. One of the biblical psalms praises God for his justice in the words:

> You [Lord] rescue the poor
> > from those too strong for them,
> the poor and needy
> > from those who rob them. (Psalm 35:10)

I lay out the verse in this fashion not just to convey the poetic rhythm of the original, but to highlight the conceptual connections in the mind of the psalmist. In the first couplet, the vulnerable poor are contrasted with the socially powerful. The idea is immediately reiterated in the second poetic couplet where the powerful of the earlier line are cast as "robbers," making the point that oppressing the poor is a kind of theft.

A similar comparison between robbery and profiting from the poor is found in the Old Testament prophet Ezekiel:

> [The righteous man] does not commit robbery but gives his food to the hungry and provides clothing for the naked. He does not lend to them at interest or take a profit from them. (Ezekiel 18:7–8)

The paragraph has a deliberate A, B, A pattern: the righteous person (A) does not rob others, but rather (B) gives to the poor and need, being careful (A) never to profit at the expense of the poor. The effect of this is to draw a parallel between robbery and profiteering from the poor. The only appropriate act toward the poor—the only way to avoid robbing them—is to give food and clothing to them. This is the origin of John Calvin's idea that we break the eighth commandment if we "become wealthy through injustice," "crush the weak," or even refuse to "assist them in their need with our abundance."

One of the Old Testament prophets goes further. Having criticized the "pious" for keeping their religious fasts while continuing to "exploit all your workers," Isaiah describes the true "fast" God requires: "Is not this the kind of fasting I have chosen: to loose the chains of injustice and untie the cords of the yoke, to set the oppressed free and break every yoke? Is it not to share your food with the hungry and to provide the poor wanderer with shelter?" (Isaiah 58:3–7). The New Testament picks up this thought and instructs former thieves to amend their ways by pursuing the opposite of theft, sharing with the needy, the *true* fulfilment of the eighth commandment:

> Anyone who has been stealing must steal no longer, but must work, doing something useful with their own hands, that they may have something to share with those in need. (Ephesians 4:28)

If oppressing and neglecting the poor is a form of robbery, the decision to no longer steal entails a decision to "share with those in need."

This connection between *stealing* and *mistreating the poor* created a very curious tension in European legal reflections in the 1200s. What if a poor man, out of sheer necessity of survival, is caught stealing from someone with plenty? Well, since it is the Lord's will that none experience poverty while their neighbours enjoy luxury, such an act is not really theft. Indeed, because there was a natural "right of the poor to sustenance" in thirteenth-century canon law discussions, it could be argued that the true thief was the rich man who neglected the poor at his doorstep. There was even a push at the time to give bishops the legal power to compel a wealthy man to provide sustenance for a poor claimant. That one didn't make it into our Western laws!

On all this, see the fascinating historical account of Charles J. Reid, Jr., "The Canonistic Contribution to the Western Rights Tradition: An Historical Inquiry," *Boston College Law Review*, vol.33:37 (1995), 37–92.

BOOK NOTES

Whatever the merits of some of these early attempts to apply the teachings of Moses and Jesus to the complexities of life in the Western world, there is little doubt that these legal and moral reflections continue to influence the ethical concerns, language, and even categories of thought of our own day.

12

SAYING WHAT IS TRUE: NINTH COMMANDMENT

The concern for social justice evident in the sixth and eighth commandments spills into the ninth Commandment. Truth in speech, especially in a court of law, is a fundamental condition of a fair society. Thus, Moses proclaimed:

> You shall not give false testimony against your neighbour. (Exodus 20:16; Deuteronomy 5:20)

The expression "give false testimony" is a direct reference to the court of law. As Old Testament specialist Chris Wright puts it, "The commandment is not simply about telling the truth in general, but about telling the truth in the place where it counts most, because that is where lying can cost most—the court of law" (Wright, *Deuteronomy*, 63). The ninth commandment, in other words, concerns "perjury," the formal submission of false or misleading evidence against another. We saw that the third commandment about misusing God's name probably referred directly, though not exclusively, to a formal vow in a court of law made in the name of Yahweh. There the concern was mainly *vertical*, dishonouring God by employing his name for trivial or false ends. Here in the ninth commandment the concern is *horizontal*, harming the reputation or livelihood of others by offering sworn testimony against them.

EYE FOR EYE

In the book of Deuteronomy, which reiterates the *torah*, Moses lays out an amazing principle of punishment for perjury: anyone discovered to have given false testimony in court was to receive the same sentence which the victim of the false accusation would have received had the decision gone against him on the basis of the false testimony. In other words, if you were accused of stealing a goat because of my deceit and I was found out, I would be forced to pay the penalty—financial or otherwise—for the theft of a goat. This is one of the contexts in which we hear those famous, often misunderstood, words, "eye for eye, tooth for tooth, hand for hand, foot for foot" (Deuteronomy 19:21). It is a call for proportionality in punishing false testimony in a court of law.

"Testimony" is the foundation of much of the legal judgments made in court. I remember talking with a friend in the final few weeks of his battle with cancer. A former judge, James had become convinced that the Gospel records of Jesus's life had the ring of "good testimony," he said. And then he marveled at the importance of testimony throughout his legal career. People he had fined and put away, others he had set free: all on the basis of sound testimony. Testimony is precious because it can determine the course of a person's life—and people are precious. Thus,

"It's absolutely central to the criminal justice system," said lawyer Robert Stary in a report on perjury on ABC Radio National, "that when a person gives their evidence on oath and it's false evidence, and it's proved to be false evidence, then once that's revealed it invariably carries a jail sentence." The report focused on the notorious case of Lord Jeffrey Archer, the novelist and one-time politician. He sued the London Tabloid *The Daily Star* for airing claims he had sex with a prostitute. He won and received over a million dollars in damages. But it turns out he had given false testimony, fabricating diaries that contradicted the newspaper's allegations. Archer was jailed for four years. It is an important principle: giving false testimony against your neighbour— *even if it is a tabloid*— perverts justice and so demands a serious penalty. Given the income Lord Archer was on, four years in jail was a significantly greater penalty than the one million dollars *The Daily Star* had been wrongly forced to pay. In this case, the British courts probably went beyond the instructions of Moses. In the US state of California the Mosaic legislative principle of "eye for eye" in perjury cases is still on the books for extreme cases: "Every person who, by willful perjury or subornation of perjury procures the conviction and execution of any innocent person, is punishable by death or life imprisonment without possibility of parole" (California, Penal Code Section 128).

"You shall not bear false witness against your neighbour" underlines the seriousness of formal, sworn testimony in a court of law. It is a fundamental principle of a fair society. That is the "shadow," but what is the "reality" behind the ninth commandment, according to the New Testament?

THE LINK BETWEEN PERJURY AND LYING

Jesus attached the same seriousness to *all* speech, inside and outside the court of law. Any "yes" or "no" ought to carry the force of the most extreme oath imaginable. In laying out his Moses-like vision of the Good in the Sermon on the Mount, Jesus declared:

> "You have heard that it was said to the people long ago, 'Do not break your oath, but fulfill to the Lord the vows you have made.' But I tell you, do not swear an oath at all: either by heaven, for it is God's throne; or by the earth, for it is his footstool; or by Jerusalem, for it is the city of the Great King. And do not swear by your head, for you cannot make even one hair white or black. All you need to say is simply 'Yes' or 'No'; anything beyond this comes from the evil one." (Matthew 5:33 – 37)

Jesus's brother James echoed the same sentiment in a letter he penned some years later:

> Above all, my brothers and sisters, do not swear — not by heaven or by earth or by anything else. All you need to say is a simple "Yes" or "No." Otherwise you will be condemned. (James 5:12)

The call for honesty in personal dealings was not an invention of the new covenant. The Old Testament certainly insists, "Do not lie. Do not deceive one another" (Leviticus 19:11). The startling thing in the teaching of Jesus was the insistence that, for his followers, there should be no such principle as *heightened* truth telling. A simple "yes" or "no" ought to have the same veracity as the most extreme form of sworn testimony. And since oaths were frequently used to justify *grades* of truthfulness, oaths should be avoided completely, he said.

Jesus's critique of oaths was unique in antiquity (so far as we can tell), but it was also a radical challenge to the legal code of his day. By the first century an elaborate system of oath swearing had developed in which truthfulness could be graded according to the type of oath given. Swearing by the gold of the Jerusalem Temple, for instance, or by some of the utensils used in the Temple, was considered *fully binding*. Swearing by Jerusalem, on the other hand, or simply by the Temple itself, was regarded as a *non-binding* oath (see the Mishnah *Nedarim* 1:3; *Shabuot* 4:13; *Sanhedrin* 3:2). The result of this system was that low-level oaths could be used to avoid telling the truth. It is in this context that Jesus rejected the first-century oath system. What counted for Jesus were not regulations about grades of truth telling but commitment to the simple principle of honesty: "All you need to say is simply 'Yes,' or 'No.'" The final line is astonishing in its ancient context. According to Jesus, the system of oath making current in first-century Judaism was "from the evil one," that is, from the devil. It's hard to imagine a harsher critique of the traditions of the Pharisees.

THE LINK BETWEEN TRUTH AND JUSTICE

Perjury is an obvious injustice. But so is lying in ordinary life. I will leave aside the topic of "white lies" and the ethical chestnut of whether it was right to lie to Nazis in WWII about Jewish friends hiding in the cellar. Think for a moment about why we lie in normal circumstances and what it says about us and about those we deceive. Most lies seem to be about deriving an invalid benefit for myself, perhaps to protect my honour, to maintain a boast, to avoid punishment, to win an argument, to rip someone off, and so on. A lie tends to belittle the deceived. It commoditizes them for my benefit. John Calvin reckoned that even "fawning politeness" broke the ninth commandment, for those who "crave praise for their witticisms" frequently do so at the expense of another's comfort or reputation (*Institutes*, Book 2, 8.48). According to the New Testament, *all the world* has the status of a court of law.

In all of this, we see how the Old Testament comes into sharp focus in the New Testament, how the shadow becomes a reality. "You shall not murder" speaks of a deeper call to refuse to denigrate those made in God's image and loved by him. "You shall not commit adultery" asks us never to direct sexual desire toward someone other than our spouse. "You shall not steal" urges us never to take or withhold what is due to another, especially those in need. And "You shall not give false testimony" demands that we shun the injustice of lying at every level of life.

NEGATIVE GRAMMAR, POSITIVE MORALITY

Before turning in the final chapter to the unusual tenth commandment, I want to offer a brief thought about the "thou shalt not" commands. People often point out that the negative form of the instructions of Moses signals a negative approach to ethics, and to life in general: "no" to this, "no" to that, religion has a reputation for denying things. And in the ten brief commands we are exploring, the Hebrew particle *lo* or "no/not" appears no fewer than thirteen times. An atheist friend on social media recently thought he had a strong case when he pointed out that being told what you're *not allowed to do* all the time sounds like the antithesis of freedom. In a human relationship, say, between parents and children, being told constantly what you are *not* to do or what you should *not* have done is extremely unhealthy. An excellent leadership book I read recently insisted that organisations should convey five positive statements for every one negative statement in order to maintain a healthy culture (Kim Cameron, *Positive Leadership: Strategies for Extraordinary Performance* [Berrett-Koehler, 2012]). The Ten Commandments certainly fail that test.

The French atheist Michel Onfray relentlessly attacks religion on precisely this point: it is the great naysayer of the world. The section headings of chapter 1 of his *Atheist Manifesto* say it all: "Monotheism's somber vision," "Down with intelligence," "Litany of taboos," and so on. In a climactic passage on the basic negativity of religion, he declares with all the certainty of a preacher:

> Religion proceeds from the death wish. That strange dark force in the depths of our being works toward the destruction of what is. Wherever life begins to move, expand, vibrate, a countercurrent sets in, tending to arrest the newborn movement and immobilize its ebb and flow. As soon as life fights its way out of the tunnel, death is there, ready to start the clock ticking—that is its function, its modus operandi—and to collapse all life's hopes and

plans.... Fired by the same inborn death drive, the three monotheisms share a series of identical forms of aversion: hatred of reason and intelligence; hatred of freedom; hatred of all books in the name of one book alone; hatred of sexuality, women, and pleasure; hatred of the feminine; hatred of the body, of desires, of drives. (Michel Onfray, *The Atheist Manifesto* [Arcade Publishing, 2005], 67)

It is stirring stuff, and I bet it sounds even stronger in the French original. But is it fair? And does the negative formulation of most of the Ten Commandments — *thou shalt not murder, steal, etc.* — provide a linguistic window into a basically deleterious approach to life?

I have said already that the Bible deliberately distances itself from the capricious view of earthly life common in the ancient Near East. This is why the opening chapter of Jewish and Christian Scripture declares everything "good" seven times (Genesis 1). The starting point of the Judeo-Christian worldview is not the *fall* of the world but its inherent worth, order, pleasure, and goodness. So how do the Ten Commandments with their thirteen *No*s fit into this positive vision of the *Good*? Put simply, we must not confuse an ethical stance with sentence grammar. The Ten Commandments are stated negatively precisely because the biblical approach to life is so positive. A few things are forbidden, because pretty much everything else is to be enjoyed.

Imagine if it were otherwise. Imagine if the commandments sought to itemize, with positive sentence grammar, all the things we were in fact permitted to do. It would fill a library with endless tomes on *Things Permitted at Home*, and *Activities Tolerated at Work*, and *Foods You May Enjoy*, and *Outings Acceptable for Families,* and *Behaviour Endorsed for Days Off,* and on it would go until every conceivable human exploit was prescribed by divine law. By contrast, the "thou shalt nots" of Moses, and the pinpoint interpretations of Jesus, may carry the *grammar* of negation, but they are imbued with a *spirit of pure freedom.* "The truth is," wrote the great British thinker G. K. Chesterton, "that the curtness of the Commandments is an evidence, not of the gloom and narrowness of a religion, but, on the contrary, of its liberality and humanity." How so? Chesterton answers: "It is shorter to state the things forbidden than the things permitted; precisely because most things are permitted, and only a few things are forbidden" (*The Complete Works of G K Chesterton* [Ignatius Press, 1989], 32:18).

The very first commandment narrated in the Bible conveys the very same logic. In the beautiful imagery of Genesis 2, the Lord sends Adam into the garden of Eden with the freedom to explore everything in God's good world, except *one* item:

> The LORD God took the man and put him in the Garden of Eden to work it and take care of it. And the LORD God commanded the man, "You are free to eat from any tree in the garden; but you must not eat from the tree of the knowledge of good and evil, for when you eat from it you will certainly die." (Genesis 2:15 – 17)

Michel Onfray exploits this passage in an attempt to prove that the Bible opposes knowledge: "You can do anything in this magnificent Garden," he says in a caricature of God's command, "except become intelligent" (*The Atheist*

Manifesto, 68). But as I have explained in my *Doubter's Guide to the Bible*, the "knowledge of good and evil" in this passage has nothing to do with comprehending the world. This tree represents—and I do believe it is picture language—the *determination* of good and evil. The decision to eat of this tree is the decision of mankind to define right and wrong without reference to the Creator. In any case, the point I want to make is a simpler one. There was a single prohibition in the garden precisely because everything else was there to be enjoyed.

The negative grammar of the Ten Commandments is a function of the Bible's liberality. So long as we avoid diminishing our Maker, working ourselves into the ground, denigrating and deceiving our neighbours, and betraying fundamental family ties, life is there to be enjoyed. Indeed, it is probably truer to say that it is only by avoiding these things that life can truly be enjoyed. God's negations are like the orange flags marking the rough patches on a ski slope. When I'm looking down my beloved Mount Perisher—barely a "mountain" by European or American standards—I don't want to be directed to the hundred or so possible routes I could take down the slope. I just want to know the few places I should avoid so I can get on with the freedom of carving up the hill.

The *Nos* of the Ten Commandments and of Jesus remind us where it is not safe to tread so that we can get on with enjoying life in God's good world. Viewed this way, even the most negatively phrased demand in the Bible is a marker of freedom.

13

FAILING AND FINDING THE GOOD: *TENTH COMMANDMENT*

To appreciate the force of the tenth commandment against "coveting" we need to jump forward in the Old Testament to that significant statement I have quoted several times already. The prophet Jeremiah, six centuries after Moses, looked back on Israel's efforts to obey the One who had rescued them from Egypt and given them the *torah* and he declared the original covenant *broken*. A new covenant was on its way:

> "The days are coming," declares the LORD, "when I will make a new covenant with the people of Israel and with the people of Judah. It will not be like the covenant I made with their ancestors when I took them by the hand to lead them out of Egypt, because they broke my covenant, though I was a husband to them," declares the LORD. "This is the covenant I will make with the people of Israel after that time," declares the LORD. "I will put my law in their minds and write it on their hearts. I will be their God, and they will be my people. No longer will they teach their neighbour, or say to one another, 'Know the LORD,' because they will all know me, from the least

of them to the greatest," declares the LORD. "For I will forgive their wickedness and will remember their sins no more." (Jeremiah 31:31–34)

Here we see that the Old Testament itself says that Israel could not keep the covenant of Moses. A new agreement was necessary. This new covenant would bring two things: an internalisation of God's *torah* (instruction or law) and the freedom of his forgiveness. "I will remember their sins no more" has to be one of the most beautiful promises in the Bible.

We have also seen that Moses himself centuries earlier hinted at a new covenant by telling his people that a "new Moses" would one day come, and "you must listen to him" (Deuteronomy 18:15, 18; 34:10). More than that, in the Ten Commandments themselves we find a hint that God's people would fail his high standards and need to call upon his forgiveness and, further, that God's intention was for his people to *internalise* his law rather than just conforming outwardly to its requirements.

COVETING AND THE NEW COVENANT

It is fitting that the tenth commandment, the climax of the *torah* of Moses, should feel like a launch pad into a whole new ethical space. Unlike the external, almost manageable instructions that come before, the final commandment is deeply *internal* and pretty much *impossible*:

> You shall not covet your neighbour's house. You shall not covet [Deuteronomy has "desire"] your neighbour's

wife, or his male or female servant, his ox or donkey, or anything that belongs to your neighbour. (Exodus 20:17; Deuteronomy 5:21)

The command against "coveting" moves us beyond the externalities of idol worship, misusing God's name, avoiding theft, and so on, and speaks to our inner motivations. I can well imagine an ancient Israelite hearing the Ten Commandments for the first time and thinking, *Yes, I believe I could manage to follow one God, avoid idols and the misuse of God's name, keep the Sabbath Day, honour parents, not murder a neighbour or sleep with their spouse, as well as not steal or perjure myself.* But then come the final fifteen words, and things look very different. Just as he was thinking he could earn a gold star in God's good books, the tenth commandment reveals the impossibility of really keeping the covenant. Who can perfectly regulate desire?

The strangeness of the tenth commandment is no doubt deliberate. It is a signal within Moses's founding charter that something more is coming, something more *has* to come or else God's people are doomed to feel that the Good Life is beyond reach. And so it points us forward to the "new covenant," in which God would simultaneously forgive us and internalise the law.

"DESIRE" IN BUDDHISM AND THE BIBLE

The tenth commandment does not refer merely to *appreciating the value* of something or someone, the way I might say I love the songs of U2, adore the writing of Marilynne

Robinson, or admire the Audi A5 my friend Stephen sometimes lends me! To "covet" means to *wish to acquire* something or someone as your possession. To "desire"—used in Moses's second rendition of the commandment in Deuteronomy—refers to *a wish arising from an internal need*.

There is a powerful critique of coveting and desire at the heart of classical Buddhism. Pausing a moment to explore this might be instructive for understanding the peculiar logic of the biblical commandment. Buddha's message was that desire is the key problem in the world and relinquishing desire the solution. His logic was compelling. The starting point is the observation that people suffer (this is the first of the Four Noble Truths). Pretty much all of life was subject to suffering, in his view. In his first recorded message—the "Sermon on the Mount" of Buddhism—Prince Gautama declared:

> The Noble Truth of Suffering, monks, is this: Birth is suffering, aging is suffering, sickness is suffering, death is suffering, association with the unpleasant is suffering, dissociation from the pleasant is suffering, not to receive what one desires is suffering. (*Setting in Motion the Wheel of Truth* [Dhammacakkappavattana Sutta] Samyutta Nikaya LVI.11, from the Sutta Pitaka)

This suffering arises because we desire things (Second Noble Truth): we desire wealth and so poverty hurts us; we desire health and so sickness troubles us; we desire life and so death frightens us; we desire honour and so failure injures us; we desire intimacy and so the ups and downs of our relationships pain us. And so on. Desire traps us in a world of pain. The Third Noble Truth follows naturally from the first two. We are released from pain only when we are able to extinguish desire:

> The Noble Truth of the Cessation of Suffering is this: It is the complete cessation of that very desire, giving it up, relinquishing it, liberating oneself from it, and detaching oneself from it. (Setting in Motion the Wheel of Truth [Dhammacakkappavattana Sutta] Samyutta Nikaya LVI.11, from the Sutta Pitaka)

The rationale is hard to argue with. If a business executive can quench her desire for a promotion, she won't be emotionally affected by being overlooked by her bosses. If a boy can detach himself from his parents' love, he will be able to maintain peace even when he loses his father. The examples are endless. The point is the same: the end of desire means the end of all pain (the Fourth Noble Truth explains the "path" to the eradication of desire). Of all the religions I have studied and taught, I have always felt that Buddhism is the most fiercely rational, and yet also the one I feel least capable of following.

The biblical command against desire or coveting is quite different. The Bible does not critique "desire" per se, certainly not in the stingingly logical manner of Buddhism. After all, the language of emotion and affection abounds in Scripture. There are many things believers *are* to crave: our spouse, justice in the world, and even God himself. "As the deer pants for streams of water," says Psalm 42:1, "so my soul pants for you, my God." Or Psalm 119:20, "My soul is consumed with longing for your laws at all times." The passion of human love is similarly celebrated in Song of Songs:

Place me like a seal over your heart, like a seal on your arm; for love is as strong as death, its jealousy unyielding as the grave. It burns like blazing fire, like a mighty flame. Many waters cannot quench love; rivers cannot sweep it away. If one were to give all the wealth of one's house for love, it would be utterly scorned. (Song of Songs 8:6–7)

Even God is frequently said to be filled with passionate desire. His "jealousy" is famous — and famously misunderstood. The prophet Hosea even describes God as a wounded but patient lover whose wife (Israel) constantly pursues other lovers:

"She burned incense to the Baals; she decked herself with rings and jewelry, and went after her lovers, but me she forgot," declares the LORD. "Therefore I am now going to allure her; I will lead her into the wilderness and speak tenderly to her. There I will give her back her vineyards, and will make the Valley of Achor a door of hope. There she will respond as in the days of her youth, as in the day she came up out of Egypt. In that day," declares the LORD, "you will call me 'my husband'; you will no longer call me 'my master.'... I will betroth you to me forever; I will betroth you in righteousness and justice, in love and compassion. I will betroth you in faithfulness, and you will acknowledge the LORD." (Hosea 2:13–16, 19–20)

God's passion for his people re-emerges toward the end of Hosea:

My people are determined to turn from me. Even though they call me God Most High, I will by no means exalt them. How can I give you up, Ephraim? How can I hand you over, Israel?... My heart is changed within me; all my compassion is aroused. I will not carry out my fierce anger. (Hosea 11:7, 8–9)

Biblical faith is a passionate faith. Moses and the prophets, God himself and Jesus, would all make terrible Buddhists!

THE THREE PARTS OF MORALITY

What does "you shall not covet/desire" really mean if it is not a critique of passion per se? The tenth commandment has little to do with providing a remedy for pain and disappointment, in the Buddhist and Stoic sense. It is a call for social, spiritual, and internal harmony.

There is a *social* dimension to the tenth commandment. To "not covet" is a decision not to wish for yourself that which properly belongs to another, whether their partner, property, status, or, as the text says, "anything that belongs to your neighbour." Coveting implies a resentment at the flourishing of others—whereas God's people are to celebrate the flourishing of others. "Rejoice with those who rejoice," says the apostle Paul (Romans 12:15).

There is a *spiritual* element, too. The degree of my coveting will be inversely proportional to my satisfaction in God. In other words, the more I find fulfilment in the Creator—in knowing his ways, trusting his mercy, relying on his guidance—the less I will covet the things of creation. In this way, the tenth commandment brings us back to the first. Chris Wright puts it perfectly:

Thus the commandments come full circle. To break the tenth is to break the first. For covetousness means setting our hearts and affections on things that then take the place of God. It is not surprising, then, conversely, that a whole culture that systematically denies the transcendent by excluding the reality of the living God from the public domain, as Western societies have been doing for generations, also ends up turning covetous self-interest into a socioeconomic ideology, rationalized, euphemized, and idolized. (*Deuteronomy,* 86)

A famous government report on Australian youth made similar observations in less overt, and less religious, terms. I remember the report so well because it came out the year before my *A Sneaking Suspicion*, an attempt to explain the relevance of Christianity for teenagers. The report helped frame some of my thinking, then and now. It was published by *Australia's Commission for the Future* and its author, Richard Eckersley, remains a prominent social scientist. "Robbed of a broader meaning to our lives," he wrote, "we appear to have entered an era of mass obsession, usually with ourselves: our appearance, our health and fitness, our work, our sex lives, our children's performance, our personal development." Avowedly non-religious, Eckersley offered conclusions more at home in a sermon than a government essay: "It may be, then, the greatest wrong we are doing to our children is not the broken families or the scarcity of jobs (damaging though these are), but the creation of a culture that gives them nothing greater than themselves to believe in — no god, no king, no country" (Richard Eckersley, *Apocalypse? No!* [Commission for the Future, 1992], 14 – 15).

The Ten Commandments taught all this more than three thousand years ago. Abandoning the Creator will lead to a passion to accumulate smaller, created meanings in the hope that they can make up for the loss of the "broader meaning," to use Eckersley's euphemism. Breaking the first commandment leads organically to breaking the tenth. Coveting is both a social and a spiritual problem.

There is also an *internal* dimension to the tenth commandment. It probes beyond the external performance of my actions to the inner workings of my soul. It asks: What is my heart really set on? Outwardly, someone could appear highly ethical but beneath the surface there is a sea of craving and resentment toward others. The tenth commandment zeros in on such resentments and passions and calls on us to develop not just external morality but inward virtue.

This internalisation of the law was central to the promise of a new covenant: "I will put my law in their minds and write it on their hearts." It explains Jesus's emphasis on the heart. Much of his transposition of Moses's law can be described as the *internalisation* of *torah*. He said the injunction against worshipping idols (second commandment) includes "the love of money." The proscription against murder (sixth commandment) means we will never denigrate another. The command against adultery (seventh commandment) includes directing your sexual desire at someone other than one's spouse. And so on. The focus on the heart in the tenth commandment was at the core of Jesus's critique of the "hypocrite" and central to his emphasis on the inner source of wrongdoing:

Don't you see that whatever enters the mouth goes into the stomach and then out of the body? But the things that come out of a person's mouth come from the heart, and these defile them. For out of the heart come evil thoughts—murder, adultery, sexual immorality, theft, false testimony, slander. These are what defile a person; but eating with unwashed hands does not defile them. (Matthew 15:17–20)

In the timeless *Mere Christianity*, C. S. Lewis speaks of what he calls "the three parts of morality"—the social, the internal, and the spiritual. He employs the image of a fleet of ships that must get all three things right in order to function effectively:

There are two ways in which the human machine goes wrong. One is when human individuals drift apart from one another, or else collide with one another and do one another damage, by cheating or bullying. The other is when things go wrong inside the individual—when the different parts of him (his different faculties and desires and so on) either drift apart or interfere with one another. You can get the idea plain if you think of us as a fleet of ships sailing in formation. The voyage will be a success only, in the first place, if the ships do not collide and get in one another's way; and, secondly, if each ship is seaworthy and has her engines in good order. As a matter of fact, you cannot have either of these two things without the other. But there is one thing we have not yet taken into account. We have not asked where the fleet is trying to get to. However well the fleet sailed, its voyage would be a failure if it were meant to reach New York and actually arrived at Calcutta. Morality, then, seems to be concerned with three things. Firstly, with fair play and harmony between individuals. Secondly, with what might be called tidying up or harmonising the things inside each individual. Thirdly, with the general purpose of human life as a whole: what man was made for; what course the whole fleet ought to be on. (*Mere Christianity*, 58–59)

Secular ethics tend to focus on the *social* dimension. If it doesn't hurt another person, it must be fine. This approach tends to ignore the question of the goal of human life, in Lewis's image *where the whole thing is headed*. Sometimes there is also a neglect of virtue or the internal character of a person. It is common now to hear people say that a public leader can be a complete rat-bag in private life, so long as he serves well for the public good. This has not always been the case. There was a time when, for example, a leader's marital betrayal was seen as reason enough for someone to step down from high office. This was not mere moralism. The logic was: If "faithfulness" and "discipline" are not inner qualities of this leader, how can the public have confidence that such virtues will guide wider social decisions? It is true this old-fashioned rationale can be oppressive and unfairly employed, but there is something to it.

Religious ethics have their own, equally problematic, flaws. They are often strong on the spiritual dimension, what we are made for. But they can very frequently go astray on both the internal and the social dimensions. Religion can promote mere external piety, divorced from genuine virtue and love for others. Hence our distaste for the "religious hypocrite" I have talked so much about in this book.

The Ten Commandments are concerned with all three parts of the ethical enterprise. We are urged to find satisfaction in our Creator and his blessings. Then we are guided to honour our family and our neighbours. And, finally, the strange tenth commandment drills down to the engine room of our soul and asks, *What do we truly desire?*

THE LAW THAT FINDS US OUT

There is another important aspect of the New Testament's handling of the tenth commandment. It, too, had an impact on centuries of Christian theology and ethics.

The apostle Paul's most famous work is a letter he wrote to Christians in Rome in the 50s AD. Like many of the earliest Christians, the members of this church were either ethnically Jewish or Gentiles who had been drawn to the teaching of Moses in the synagogue before hearing about Christianity. It is one of the rarely told stories of ancient history that Jews had more than a little success in converting Greeks and Romans to Jewish ways. The early success of Christianity—humanly speaking—can be explained, in part, by the influence Judaism was already having on Gentiles (non-Jews) in the Roman world. When people like Paul came along with the "new covenant" insistence that Gentiles need not undergo Jewish circumcision in order to belong to the God of Israel, that meant the world to many Greeks and Romans (for spiritual and practical reasons!).

In his epistle to the Romans, Paul—a one-time Jewish Pharisee—urges his readers not to imagine that the law of Moses can make someone righteous in God's eyes. The law is holy and good, he says, but it cannot make us acceptable to the Almighty because none of us can obey it perfectly. Instead, we must rely on Jesus Christ, he said. He lived the perfect life none of us could. He then gave his life on a cross as the perfect sacrifice for sins. All who call on God for mercy receive his salvation. They are "righteous by faith," to use Paul's language. Only then does obedience to God's *torah*, the new *torah* taught by the new Moses, make sense. Structurally, this is identical to Moses's own teaching: the opening line of the Ten Commandments is not a call for Israel to obey God but a reminder that God had already rescued Israel. Obeying the law was to be an expression of thankfulness for the mercy already received. It was never meant to function as a moral ladder to win high standing before a holy God.

In chapter 7 of his letter to Rome, Paul drives this point home with a stunning reflection on the tenth commandment. The passage is widely discussed by New Testament scholars — in particular, whether Paul is describing his own Christian struggle to obey God or the struggle of anyone who tries to be righteous by obeying the law of Moses. For our purposes, the broad point is clear: the law of Moses, and the tenth commandment especially, exposes all of us as incapable of perfect righteousness; we must therefore cry out to God for the mercy promised in the new covenant:

> Is the law sinful? Certainly not! Nevertheless, I would not have known what sin was had it not been for the law. For I would not have known what coveting really was if the law had not said, "You shall not covet." But sin, seizing the

opportunity afforded by the commandment, produced in me every kind of coveting.... We know that the law is spiritual; but I am unspiritual, sold as a slave to sin. I do not understand what I do. For what I want to do I do not do, but what I hate I do. And if I do what I do not want to do, I agree that the law is good.... So I find this law at work: Although I want to do good, evil is right there with me. For in my inner being I delight in God's law; but I see another law at work in me, waging war against the law of my mind and making me a prisoner of the law of sin at work within me. What a wretched man I am! Who will rescue me from this body that is subject to death? Thanks be to God, who delivers me through Jesus Christ our Lord! (Romans 7:7–8, 14–16, 21–25)

As I say, the details are complicated but the wider theme is plain. Anyone who thinks they can become "good" by obedience to God's demands is destined to failure: "What a wretched man I am!" And the tenth commandment against coveting is key. For even if we think we might be able to avoid idols, not commit murder, and so on, none of us can consistently direct our desire toward the good of others. The law of Moses holds up a mirror to our soul. It exposes the heart and drives us to the cry, "Who will rescue me from this body that is subject to death?" The answer Paul gives is the answer that launched Christianity around the world: "Thanks be to God, who delivers me through Jesus Christ our Lord!"

I will never forget the young man I met after a talk I gave at his school in New South Wales. He approached me after the speech and, picking up on my mention of God in the address, he asked, "How do you know if God accepts you or not?" He showed me a small accounting book in which he had drawn columns. Down the left side was a list of ethical virtues he thought might please the Almighty — patience, kindness, politeness, and so on. Across the top of the page he had written the days of the week. Within the columns he had given himself a score out of ten for each virtue, for each day of the week, for pages and pages. He asked what I thought. I looked down at the numbers: a few 7s, quite a few 3s and 4s. His own record keeping said it all. It found him out. And the poor lad was troubled. I had the great privilege of explaining to him, right there in the schoolyard, the teaching of Jesus and Paul. God's law — especially the tenth commandment — finds us all out. But the Christian message has always been that Christ died on our behalf so that we might be freely forgiven. The record is cancelled. We are "rescued . . . from this body that is subject to death," as Paul says. That's not exactly how I put it to this teenager, but the basic point was the same. I noticed a change come across his face, and a small tear. He took the book in his hands, walked over to the playground trash can, and theatrically threw his accounting book away. In the space of 10 – 15 minutes, I watched this young man move from the cry, "What a wretched man I am!" to "thanks be to God, who delivers me through Jesus Christ our Lord!"

AUGUSTINE AND THE MAKING OF THE WEST

This profound admission of "sinfulness" and consequent reliance upon God's pure grace (prompted by the tenth commandment) are the twin themes of one of the most influential texts of early Western history. Augustine of Hippo (AD 354–430) stands as a colossus at the doorway between the classical Greco-Roman world and the Christian civilisation that emerged in medieval and early modern Europe. He was a philosopher and bishop, deeply learned in the thought of Greece and Rome and famously converted through an encounter with the New Testament letters of Paul. His writings influenced much of the *religious* thought of the next millennium, both in the Roman Catholic church and, perhaps especially, the Protestant Reformation. His account of human nature is even credited with creating the intellectual environment that led to the rise of the empirical sciences in sixteenth-century Europe. As astonishing as such a claim may sound, it is well documented and widely discussed (on this, see Peter Harrison, *The Fall of Man and the Foundations of Science* [Cambridge University Press, 2007], 52–88).

Augustine is frankly one of the most important thinkers, religious or otherwise, in Western history. And it all began with the picture of human sinfulness and divine grace in Romans 7. "Augustine's major works are landmarks in the abandonment of Classical ideals," declares the entry on him in the *Oxford Classical Dictionary*. "His early optimism was soon overshadowed by a radical doctrine of grace." This change was canonized in an autobiographical masterpiece, the *Confessions* ("Augustine," 215–16). It is from this text, the *Confessions*, that I want to offer a snapshot of Augustine's reflection on law, sin, and grace. Fittingly, he puts the passage—in fact, the entire book—in the form of an address, or confession, to God:

So now I seized greedily upon the adorable writing of
Your Spirit, and especially upon the Apostle Paul. And I
found that those difficulties, in which it had once seemed
to me that he contradicted himself and that the text of his
discourse did not agree with the testimonies of the law
and the prophets, vanished away. In that pure eloquence
I saw One Face, and I learned to rejoice with trembling.
I found that whatever truth I had read in the Platonists
[the most important Greco-Roman philosophers of late
antiquity] was said here with praise of Your grace: that he
who sees should not so glory as if he had not received—
and received, indeed, not only what he sees but even the
power to see. For though a man be delighted with the
law of God according to the inward man, what shall he
do about that other law in his members, fighting against
the law of his mind and captivating him in the law of sin
that is in his members? For Thou art just, O Lord, but we
have sinned, we have committed iniquity, we have done
wickedly and Thy hand has grown heavy upon us. But
what shall unhappy man do? Who shall deliver him from
the body of this death, save the grace of God by Jesus
Christ our Lord whom Thou has begotten coeternally
with Thee. The writings of the Platonists contain nothing
of all this. Their pages show nothing of the face of that
love, the tears of confession, Your sacrifice, an afflicted
spirit, a contrite and humble heart, the salvation of Your
people, the espoused city, the promise of the Holy Spirit,
the chalice of our redemption. Marvellously these truths
graved themselves in my heart when I read the least of
Your Apostles and looked upon Your works and trembled.
(Augustine, *Confessions* 7.21, tr. F. J. Sheed [Hackett Publishing, 2006], 136–37)

Augustine wrote some ninety-three books, but the *Confessions* captures one of his most enduring intellectual legacies, for the church and beyond. He crystallised into a coherent system both an acute awareness of our inability to attain the Good Life *and* a joyful dependence on the surpassing grace of God for all who trust him. If this juxtaposition sounds almost clichéd, it is probably because most of us are more influenced by Augustine, Paul, Jesus, and Moses than we imagine. It is a peculiarly *Western* vision of reality to see ourselves as deeply flawed creatures who are nonetheless deeply loved by the Creator. It is almost the reverse of the Greek and Roman perspective which, on the one hand, was overly optimistic about the potential of the philosophically trained soul and, on the other, terribly pessimistic about divinity. The more monotheistically minded philosophers regarded God as too remote to be known or relied upon in any personal way. Those who accepted the traditional pantheon saw the gods as fickle and frightening beings for whom humanity was a frequent annoyance. For a clear (and enjoyable) window into these things you can do no better than read Homer's *Iliad*—perhaps the most formative piece of writing in the Greco-Roman world. Whatever learned pagans thought of the historical basis of the events in this classic, they found in it a sound picture of the relation between gods and men. It was a relationship of contest, danger, and constant striving. The gift of Moses, Jesus, Paul, and Augustine to Western thought was simultaneously to proclaim our absolute defeat before the righteousness of God *and* our unimaginable exaltation because of his love for us. In acknowledging the captivity of our soul we became free. In bowing low we were lifted up. In crying, "What a wretched man I am!" we were able to shout, "Thanks be to God, who delivers me." C. S. Lewis once again gets this right:

> God may be more than moral goodness: He is not less. The road to the promised land runs past Sinai. The moral law may exist to be transcended: but there is no transcending it for those who have not first admitted its claims upon them and then tried with all their might to make that claim, and fairly and squarely faced the fact of the failure. (*Problem of Pain*, [HarperOne, 2009], 59)

All of this goes back to the tenth commandment, the signal that none of us can fully keep God's expectations and so all of us need to rely on his gift of grace. The *torah* will be broken, the prophet Jeremiah told us, but in the new covenant the Lord pledges, "I will forgive their iniquities and remember their sins no more." These twin themes of *sin* and *grace*, which were present in the Ten Commandments but fully disclosed in Jesus and Paul (and, later, Augustine), have shaped Western religion and society in several ways, positive and negative. None of the theology may be true, as I keep saying, but all of it had its effect on tendencies and attitudes peculiar to Westerners.

BOOK NOTES | For an authoritative biography of Augustine see, Peter Brown, *Augustine of Hippo: A Biography, New Edition, with an Epilogue* (University of California Press, 2000); or the much briefer one by Henry Chadwick, *Augustine: A Very Short Introduction* (Oxford University Press, 2001).

THE ABUSE OF SIN AND GRACE

It is not easy simultaneously to hold that we are deeply flawed sinners and yet objects of divine love. The temptation through history has been to emphasise one over the other, with unhelpful consequences. It is undeniable that in the history of the church the emphasis on human sinfulness has led to scandalous abuses of power as religious officials used guilt as a means of controlling those with a tender conscience. Perhaps some readers will be feeling a modern version of that right now. On the other hand, the themes of God's love and grace have also been employed in ways never intended by Moses or Jesus. Church leaders have excused themselves of abominable actions in the name of divine mercy and acceptance (I'm thinking of paedophile priests and fallen televangelists, but the examples are numerous).

A related, but quite different, version is found in the way some wings of the modern church have all but given up classical Christian convictions about sin—whether in the realm of sexual ethics or social ethics. Wider society, too, has grown weary of the notion of human "fallenness"—perhaps as a reaction to the pulpit-thumping, hell-fire preachers of yesteryear—and now feels a kind of holy outrage at any talk of "sin" in the public square. I often feel this recent phenomenon is a deeply *Christian* heresy. No self-respecting pagan would ever have had the temerity to imagine God as an entirely benevolent grandfather figure who only ever affirmed our choices. Judaism and Christianity alone of the religious traditions promoted pictures of God as the kindly father, desperate mother, and even wounded lover. These images, if not held in balance with the broader teaching of the Bible, easily lead to the inoffensive modern projection of uniformly friendly divinity.

But there is another story, one much truer to the twin themes of sin and grace emanating from the Old and New Testaments. For much of Western history, and today, believers have been able to flex two biceps at the same time: the muscle of moral conviction and the muscle of compassion for all regardless of morality. On the one hand, the ethical demands of the Ten Commandments and the rest of the Bible are clear. No one can say they follow Moses or Jesus and hold no firm convictions about power, sex, money, religion, and so on. This is why the church often comes across as strident when it comes to "right and wrong." But it would be wrong, under normal circumstances, to conclude from this that Christians were simply moralistic. On their better days, believers see themselves as flawed, like everyone else, and acceptable to God *only because of his grace*. British intellectual—and recent Christian convert—Francis Spufford writes almost humorously about this insistence that no one, not even the most devout believer, ever measures up to God's standards, and how this has positive social consequences:

> Not only is Christianity insanely perfectionist in its few positive recommendations, it's also insanely perfectionist about motive. It won't accept generosity performed for the sake of self-interest *as* generosity. It says that unless altruism is altruism all the way down, it doesn't count as altruism at all. So far, so thrillingly impractical. But now notice the consequence of having an ideal of behaviour not sized for human lives: everyone fails. Really *everyone*. No one

only means well, no one means well all the time. Looked at from this perspective, human beings all exhibit different varieties of f***-up. And suddenly in its utter lack of realism Christianity becomes very realistic indeed, intelligently resigned to our vast array of imperfections and much more interested in what we can do to live with them than in laws designed to keep them segregated. Christianity maintains no register of clean and unclean. It doesn't believe in the possibility of clean, just as it doesn't believe that laws can ever be fully adequate, or that goodness can reliably be achieved by following an instruction book. (*Unapologetic: Why, Despite Everything, Christianity Can Still Make Surprising Emotional Sense* [HarperOne, 2014], 45–46)

This means that healthy Christians are able simultaneously to flex both biceps. They can have strong opinions about ethics and religion and yet treat with respect and friendship the (in their view) unethical and irreligious. They can, as the cliché goes, hate the sin and love the sinner. After all, they do it with themselves all the time. We all do. We all recognise our failings and foibles, but we don't have any difficulty feeding ourselves, making sure we're well treated, and hoping other people will like us. "I do not think that I love myself because I am particularly good," C. S. Lewis once wrote, "but just because I am myself and quite apart from my character.... You dislike what you have done, but you don't cease to love yourself" (*God in the Dock* [Eerdmans, 2014], 37). That's how any genuine follower of Jesus is being trained to see others: flawed and beloved.

Jesus was the master at flexing these two muscles. He could lament that "out of the heart come evil thoughts—murder, adultery, sexual immorality, theft, false testimony, slander," and then he could sit down at the dinner table with all the "sinners":

> Then Levi held a great banquet for Jesus at his house, and a large crowd of tax collectors and others were eating with them. But the Pharisees and the teachers of the law who belonged to their sect complained to his disciples, "Why do you eat and drink with tax collectors and sinners?" Jesus answered them, "It is not the healthy who need a doctor, but the sick. I have not come to call the righteous, but sinners to repentance." (Luke 5:29–32)

It was precisely the first Christians' knowledge that they were "sinners saved by grace," to use a theological cliché, that allowed them to walk through the Roman world, with its shocking excesses of sex and violence, with a cheerful moral conviction and compassion for all. On any given day you might have thought of the ancient church as "right-wing moralists" or as "weak-willed lefties," to use modern caricatures. They were neither, of course. They just believed in sin and grace.

THE DOCTRINE OF GRACE AND THE TRADITION OF INDISCRIMINATE CARE

All of this had practical consequences. I have spoken before of the church's unusual tradition of charitable works, inherited from Jewish communities before them. The truly remarkable thing was the way Christians seemed to have opened up this care to Jew and Gentile alike, to saint and sinner alike (because ultimately there was no difference). In the second century a Roman leader urged wealthy believers to use their money to assist widows and orphans and even to purchase mistreated slaves in the neighbourhood and bring them into their own households (*Shepherd of Hermas* 50.7). I should say that at this stage Christians were not in a position to end slavery per se, but they did what they could to mitigate its effects.

A century or two later, emperor Julian provides clear evidence that Christian aid was indiscriminate, available to believer and unbeliever alike. In a letter of AD 362 bemoaning the rise of Christianity he complained: "the impious Galileans support not only their own poor but ours as well" (Julian, *Letter 22, To Arcacius*). In the following century, the churches in the tip of North Africa—under the direction of the great Augustine himself—were conducting regular raids to free slaves being shipped through local ports (*Augustine's Advice to Alypius, Epistle 10*, AD 428). There was no question that such assistance was for all, regardless of race, religion, or morality. Augustine and his fellow bishops were also roundly criticised by provincial governors for their other habit of interceding on behalf of condemned prisoners. In one letter he politely pointed out to the authorities: "It is easy and simple to hate evil men because they are evil, uncommon and dutiful to love them because they are men; thus in one and the same person you disapprove the guilt and approve the nature" (Augustine, *Epistle* 153.3). Another version of the same double principle is found in the eleventh-century view of how to treat poor thieves. The great canon jurists of Europe—these are the legal and moral minds of mother church at the height of Christendom—argued that those caught stealing to survive were exempt from prosecution, as I earlier noted. We often associate the Middle Ages with relentless brutality, but this idea of medieval barbarism is more fable than history.

BOOK NOTES | Important works on this much-overlooked period I have referred to numerous times include Brian Tierney, *Western Europe in the Middle Ages, 300–1475* (McGraw Hill, 1999); and Peter Brown, *The World of Late Antiquity: AD 150–750* (Norton, 2013).

One of my favourite examples of the church's ability to maintain moral conviction while extending compassion to all comes from the first years of the founding of Australia. In establishing the penal colony of New South Wales in 1788, the British government in its wisdom sent a chaplain with the First Fleet. His role was to serve the religious needs of the 900 convicts, marines, and settlers. It was generally hoped he might be able to civilise many through moral instruction. They chose Richard Johnson, a Cambridge-trained Anglican priest of the evangelical wing of the church. He was a friend of the former slave trader and convert John Newton (of "Amazing Grace" fame) and the great anti-slavery campaigner William Wilberforce. Like his colleagues, he was a devout moral reformer and a man of supreme grace. Johnson saw no contradiction between preaching the Christian gospel and serving the public good.

He engaged with convicts and officers alike. Refusing to play the role of moral policeman, as successive governors had hoped, he sought to convey Christ's grace even to the most irreligious and immoral.

Following the terrible outbreak of sickness on the Second Fleet of 1789, Johnson, against all advice, visited the diseased and putrid holds of ships where convicts lay listless and abandoned. The official *Australian Dictionary of Biography* entry on Johnson notes how one convict wrote home to his relatives, "few of the sick would recover if it was not for the kindness of the Rev. Mr. Johnson, whose assistance out of his own stores makes him the physician both of soul and body" (the full entry is well worth reading and is available online: http://adb.anu.edu.au). My point here is that Johnson embodied a principle that was *not* unusual in the history of Christianity. He was a moralist and a humanitarian. He held robust convictions about sex, violence, drinking, and so on, but in the first decade of British settlement in Australia no name was more closely associated with the love of God and neighbour than the Reverend Mr. Johnson. It was a message he was able to convey to all, including perhaps the first Christian convert on Australian soil, Samuel Peyton, a twenty-one-year-old thief who was hanged within six months of the First Fleet's arrival in 1788. Peyton wrote home to his mother the night before his execution with the "help of a commiserating friend," expressing a profound sense of his own wrongdoing and equally profound trust in God's grace. "I have at length fallen," he writes, "an unhappy, though just, victim to my own follies." And, yet, "For these and all my other transgressions, however great, I supplicate the Divine forgiveness; and encouraged by the promises of that Saviour who died for us all, I trust to receive that mercy in the world to come, which my offences have deprived me of in this." It fell to the Reverend Richard Johnson to guide the young Peyton through his final distressing days and hours. It is not too much to suggest that in the ministry of Johnson and the words of a young convict we see the influence across time and space of Moses, Jesus, and Paul (and even Augustine).

I titled this final chapter "Failing and Finding the Good" because the tenth commandment both fails us and, to the degree that we give up our sense of goodness and depend instead on God's grace, it frees us to know the love of God in Christ. The Christian life is free from the striving of the pure moralist. But it is also free from the aimless amorality of the modern libertarian. Those who listen to Moses, Jesus, and Paul know what God demands, recognise they can't really do it, call on God for his mercy, and then find themselves free to pursue the Good Life without fear of judgment or personal disappointment. The life of the "new covenant" is lived with a profound sense of exposure before God's law, a profound gratitude for the mercy of God in Jesus, and a profound desire to live God's way in the power of the Holy Spirit. "The fruit of the Spirit," said the apostle Paul to his Galatian churches, "is love, joy, peace, forbearance, kindness, goodness, faithfulness, gentleness and self-control. Against such things there is no law" (Galatians 5:22–23).

For readers who find they cannot share these theological convictions, I would add that there is still some benefit in understanding these ideas that have influenced the world as we know it. On the one hand, it might help you to distinguish a real believer from a "hypocrite." And I hope I have inspired some to take up the secular-Christian challenge to expose hypocrisy wherever it is found. It will be doing us all a favour.

I also hope I have made clear that Christian moral convictions are not always motivated by a judgmental spirit; they are not a sign of a loss of the humanitarian spirit. In fact, this should never be the case. Next time you hear some believer in the media, or just down at the pub, express an ethical viewpoint that sounds to the modern ear like moralism, ask yourself—no, ask them—"Don't you think it's possible to profoundly disagree with someone's morality and profoundly love them all the same?" If they say, *No*, you may have found yourself a hypocrite. If they say, *Yes*—and demonstrate that love in their lives—you have found a believer, and you will probably surprise them by having articulated the inner secret of their Christian life.

AFTERWORD TO THE FOREWORD OF THE TEN COMMANDMENTS

I want to close, perhaps oddly, with a grammatical observation that turns out to be deeply personal. It comes from the Foreword to the Ten Commandments, but it fits well here at the end.

It is quite clear that the Ten Commandments are directed at each of us individually. In Deuteronomy there is a striking shift from the plural pronoun "you" in the preamble to the commandments to the singular "you" throughout the commandments themselves (in both renditions). Let me quote Moses's foreword to the commandments employing the colloquial Australianism "yous" — Southerners in the US can read y'all:

> The LORD our God made a covenant with us at Horeb. It was not with our ancestors that the LORD made this covenant, but with us, with all of us who are alive here today. The LORD spoke to *yous* face to face out of the fire on the mountain. (At that time I stood between the LORD and *yous* to declare to *yous* the word of the LORD, because *yous* were afraid of the fire and did not go up the mountain.) And he said: "I am the LORD *your* [suddenly singular] God, who brought *you* [singular] out of Egypt,

out of the land of slavery. *You* [singular] shall have no other gods before me. *You* [singular] shall not make for *yourself* [singular] an image. (Deuteronomy 5:2 – 8)

The benefit of using an old English translation, such as the King James Version, is that you can observe the grammatical shift that is there in the original Hebrew: from the plural "The LORD talked with *you*" ("you" is always plural in old English) to the archaic singular, "I am the LORD *thy* God, which brought *thee* out of the land of Egypt, from the house of bondage. *Thou* shalt have none other gods before me," and so on through all ten.

The point of this grammatical observation is not just technical accuracy. It is that God addresses you and me *personally* in the Ten Commandments. We are not meant to generalize our reading of the commandments into a discussion about the kind of society we want, or about how far our nation has fallen from God's standards, and all that. Nor are we to theorize about the person we really wish was hearing this message (or reading this book). The Ten Commandments are personal. They are addressed to each of us. They speak to me, and to *thee*.

Doubter's Guide to the Bible

Inside History's Bestseller for Believers and Skeptics

John Dickson

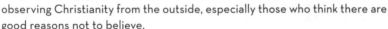

A Doubter's Guide to the Bible is a concise account of the whole biblical narrative and the lifestyle it inspires, representing a unique and engaging framework for those observing Christianity from the outside, especially those who think there are good reasons not to believe.

In this book, Dickson provides a readable and winsome Bible primer summarizing the main themes in scripture, and addresses tough questions such as "How can we read the creation account in Genesis in light of modern science?" and, "how do we approach Old Testament law when it appears inconsistent and irrelevant?"

By presenting the whole of the Bible as an account of God's promise to restore humanity to Himself, and humanity to one another and to creation, Dickson allows believers and skeptics alike to gain insight into why the Bible has been a compelling, life-changing, and magnetic force throughout the ages.

Available in stores and online!

The Christ Files

How Historians Know What They Know about Jesus

John Dickson

In *The Christ Files*, a four-session small group Bible study, scholar John Dickson examines the Christian faith through a historical look at the Christian faith and life of Jesus from both scriptural and other non-Bible documentation.

Unique among the world's religions, the central claims of Christianity concern not just timeless spiritual truths but tangible historical events as well. Historian John Dickson examines Christianity's claims in the light of history, opening you and your group to a wealth of ancient sources and explaining how mainstream scholars—whether or not they claim Christian faith personally—reach their conclusions about history's most influential figure, Jesus of Nazareth.

The Christ Files will help you and your small group expand your understanding of early Christianity and the life of Jesus.

This 110-page participant guide includes seven chapters of reading and background contextual information, along with questions for four impactful small group sessions. It is meant for use in conjunction with the four-session *The Christ Files* DVD (sold separately).

Available in stores and online!

ZONDERVAN®
.com

Life of Jesus

Who He Is and Why He Matters

John Dickson

What really happened back in the first century, in Jerusalem and around the Sea of Galilee, that changed the shape of world history? Who is this figure who emerges from history to have a profound impact on culture, ethics, politics, and philosophy? Join historian John Dickson on this journey through the life of Jesus.

This book, which features a self-contained discussion guide for use with *Life of Jesus* DVD (available separately), will help you and your friends dig deeper into what is known about Jesus's life and why it matters.

"John Dickson has done a marvelous job of presenting the story of Jesus, and the full meaning of that story, in a way that is both deeply faithful to the biblical sources and refreshingly relevant to tomorrow's world and church. I strongly recommend this study to anyone who wants to re-examine the deep historical roots of Christian faith and to find them as life-giving as they ever were."—Tom Wright

Available in stores and online!

Best Kept Secret of Christian Mission

Promoting the Gospel with More Than Our Lips

John Dickson

This book comes out of years of reflection, failures, and some successes in the task of reaching out to others with the gospel.

In this practical guide to the biblical art of sharing your faith, John Dickson offers refreshing insight into the ways that all Christians can and should be involved in spreading the good news of Jesus. While not all Christians are called and gifted to become evangelists, we are all called to promote the gospel through a wide range of activities—prayer, financial partnership, good deeds, godly lives, public worship, daily conversation, etc.—with and without our lips.

As readers engage with this book, grapple with its arguments, and hear the stories of people coming to faith, they will be inspired to see the whole of life as significant for bringing the gospel to the world, and they will be liberated out of guilt and self-consciousness in evangelism into becoming perfectly natural promoters of Jesus Christ.

Available in stores and online!

Humilitas

A Lost Key to Life, Love, and Leadership

John Dickson

Humility, or holding power loosely for the sake of others, is sorely lacking in today's world. Without it, many people fail to develop their true leadership potential and miss out on genuine fulfillment in their lives and their relationships. *Humilitas: A Lost Key to Life, Love, and Leadership* shows how the virtue of humility can turn your strengths into true greatness in all areas of life. Through the lessons of history, business, and the social sciences, author John Dickson shows that humility is not low self-esteem, groveling, or losing our distinct gifts. Instead, humility both recognizes our inherent worth and seeks to use whatever power we have at our disposal on behalf of others. Some of the world's most inspiring and influential players have been people of immense humility. The more we learn about humility, the more we understand how essential it is to a satisfying career and personal life. By embracing this virtue, we will transform for good the unique contributions we each make to the world.

Available in stores and online!